Somewhere The Train Goes:

A Life Journey

James P. O'Brien

© 2016

Table of Contents

Preface		page v
Chapter 1	**California, We Are Gone**	page 1
Chapter 2	**The Rain in Drain**	page 7
Chapter 3	**Rustic Setting in Yoncalla**	page 16
Chapter 4	**Shampoo with the Crews**	page 19
Chapter 5	**Too Much Talent**	page 24
Chapter 6	**Pea-ing in Milton-Freewater**	page 29
Chapter 7	**Never Hesitate: Just Fumigate**	page 32
Chapter 8	**Unknown Garrett at Barrett**	page 36
Chapter 9	**Enhance Household Finance**	page 43
Chapter 10	**Last Resort: Move To Dallesport**	page 54
Chapter 11	**On Mosier, On Mosier**	page 64
Chapter 12	**Dilettante With Many Instruments**	page 76
Chapter 13	**Halting Steps Toward Adulthood**	page 82
Chapter 14	**Nervous Over Military Service**	page 86
Chapter 15	**Music Maestro and Math Mentor**	page 89
Chapter 16	**Ph. D. = Piled Higher and Deeper**	page 93
Chapter 17	**Dream Job, For A While**	page 97
Chapter 18	**Why Hesitate: Just Emigrate**	page 103
Chapter 19	**Redefinition: A 28-Year Objective**	page 116
Chapter 20	**It's a Dog's Life**	page 130
Chapter 21	**Let's Get Away From It All**	page 138
Chapter 22	**Socializing in Social Security City**	page 148
Chapter 23	**Can't Spend It All**	page 156
Chapter 24	**Then, Now and To Be**	page 160
Acknowledgements		page 167
Copyright		page 169
About the Author		page 170

Preface

A good deal of my life has been anticipating the next move. When I was 12 years old, in late afternoon after I had finished my chores, I would walk my dog, Happy, a small fox terrier, below our Mosier home and sit on the rocks above the railroad tracks. U.S. Highway 30 was above me, the Union Pacific rail line and Columbia River below me. Everyone was going somewhere, whether by truck, car, train or boat. And here I sat.

Greyhound and Trailways buses traveled old Highway 30, passengers moving east and west. Where were they going? I would wait for the passenger train out of Portland in late afternoon to pass my vantage point, travelers sitting comfortably in the lounge car, others having dinner. Where were they going? The freight trucks that always seemed either to shift up or down near where I was perched carried goods to unknown points in both directions. Where would they unload? Even the Tidewater tugs and barges far out in the river, traveling both directions, were going somewhere. Where? No one seemed to be stopping or staying in Mosier.

This fascination with three modes of transportation I observed, road, rail and river, have defined my life. If I landed in one spot for any period of time, I was eventually on the move somewhere. Moving on was my earliest memory. That continual compulsion to travel is still part and parcel of my persona seven decades later.

I've titled this memoir "Somewhere The Train Goes: A Life Journey". Somewhere? My story provides the answer. Whenever I am with my brother or sister, I listen to them tell a story about those travels and their childhood, about their lives, about our parents, about high school. It always begins "Do you remember when we were kids and . . . " I rarely interrupt neither to diffuse their excitement about the past nor interject a story myself, thinking it is good therapy for them to remember the past and weigh how it made them who they are today.

As for my younger relatives and friends, if I start a story and take a breath, the story morphs without transition to one of theirs, so I still end up listening. His or her life is much more exciting than mine could ever have been and no one wants to listen to an old person's story. For even younger folks, however, there are no stories to tell. Reporting is all done on Facebook so they can garner 563 "likes" daily from their 1258 friends for washing their car, eating a taco or flushing a toilet. There is no narrative, no continuity, no interpretation, but, rather, a series of disconnected word bites and "selfies" that are posted on the Internet immediately for the world's entertainment, delight, comment and envy. I doubt they will ever have a family photo album either.

When I attend a class reunion, and for me that is rarely, similarly it is mostly "do you remember . . .?" There is always a story, sometimes even true but certainly augmented over time, which I have heard before. But I don't counter with my own story. I can't top that.

It is much like this even now visiting with friends over the dinner table. I listen to their endeavors and adventures, asking questions about this and that, to avoid having to tell my own stories. I simply don't share unless I am directly asked and then in the most laconic manner.

In all these situations, I seldom am able to express inner thoughts and feelings about something I am doing or did in the past or why it made me who and what I am today. I have always looked to the future to do the next thing, to read the next book, to learn a new concept, to travel to the new place or to enjoy the next experience.

But now it's my turn. All those stories I never got to tell I am going to tell right here. I don't even know why but I'm going to do it. As I began to write, I could not believe how fertile my memory is, remembering events, names, dates, smells and even feelings from 70-plus years ago in a pretty accurate chronology. It's not world history but it is a dialogue with myself about myself. What is strange, however, is how memory changes as one ages. I sometimes forget the five items I was to fetch from the grocery store or why I entered a room, but I can detail the late afternoon of December 16, 1951 or the sunrise on April 3, 1972.

I know so many people who say they should write a book about their life. They probably should, but they never do. I have never said I should write a book about my life, but I just have.

So, reader beware!

Maybe this is my life flashing before me and I have already died. Perhaps these memories will now be flushed from my mind forever thanks to my speedy computer and the hard drive in my head. At least they are now recorded and maybe one or two people will read them. Better to read it here than in the numerous diaries I have kept over the years, which I can now destroy. They probably would never have landed in the Library of Congress anyway. The Mosier Library? Probably not there, either.

Whatever the case, I've had great fun reminiscing to myself about myself as well as about my relatives and friends while choosing the correct expressions to capture those experiences. I love to write. I think I have been able to weigh judgments I've made along the way and to say "This is why I am the way I am and why I believe what I believe." There are inherent biases, like we all have, based on where, how and when we lived, if not why.

But I also look back and realize I was greatly blessed in so many ways and continue to be. There was never deprivation, only privilege. Privilege to be raised in one family and always to be nurtured, physically, psychologically and mentally most of the time. Privilege to be married to one person who I loved for over 43 years. Perhaps this writing is merely a way to thank my parents, my siblings, my friends, my spouse, but mostly God for my good life and now seek redemption for the bad things I've thought and done. I do not believe God waits to reward or punish you, depending on where you are in your life, but He uses your situations to shape you continually into what you should be. Perhaps this memoir is part of His great plan for me.

And the life has been very good. As an ordinary person, I've had a pretty extraordinary life and it's not over yet. I hope you read about it and it would be nice, but not essential, that you enjoy it. And I particularly hope I am not dead.

James (Jim) P. O'Brien
February 2016
Tucson, AZ

Chapter 1   California, We Are Gone

My earliest memory is returning from church on December 7, 1941, and hearing my father exclaim the Imperial Japanese Navy and Air Service [1] had bombed Pearl Harbor [2] and we would soon be at war. In truth, he did not quite say it that way, but used the derogatory racial slur [3] common during World War II. He then called his stepfather, Grandpa Powers, and said: "Turn on the radio!" President Roosevelt declared war on Japan the following day, with the European declarations a few days after that. My mother immediately burst into tears, an emotional response that occurred many times without much provocation. I was three months away from being three years old, but I remember it vividly. They say a child's earliest memories are always connected to the emotions around him or her at the time. [4] The emotions were high.

Days later, my memory was centered on the Big Ben alarm clock with luminescent numerals and hands that glowed in the dark.   In the darkness of the night, my sister said it looked just like the enemy, glaring at us and they were coming to get little boys. We certainly used the ethnically charged word [5] in those days and were not concerned with racial designations that were not necessarily politically correct. This was particularly true if it referred to the enemy. Fortunately, that has all changed. [6]

The family was crouched in the little Lomita house in California, waiting for the air raid to end, all lights out. Many nights we all slept in the same bed during blackouts. Mom said if we were going to die from a bomb, at least we would all be together. I was frightened. At times, the Los Angeles searchlights combed the skies overhead and we thought we saw aircraft, probably Mitsubishi A6Ms, [7] ready to bomb our city. We lived right near the waterfront, a strategic area, knowing the devastation of Pearl Harbor. All the houses on our street were dark but some neighbors and probably my father were in the streets, watching the skies. Rumors were rampant and we all feared an invasion. Someone had said the Japanese would take all the young children from their families and I was a young child.

---

[1] https://en.wikipedia.org/wiki/Imperial_Japanese_Navy
[2] http://www.eyewitnesstohistory.com/pearl.htm
[3] https://en.wikipedia.org/wiki/Jap
[4] https://answers.yahoo.com/question/index?qid=20140723131130AAUduAs
[5] http://www.japan-talk.com/jt/new/is-the-word-Jap-derogatory
[6] http://www.funnyordie.com/articles/4869b8b21e/to-avoid-future-confusion-here-is-a-list-of-racial-slurs?_cc=S_d__&_ccid=o8ciji.o08c6j
[7] http://www.militaryfactory.com/aircraft/pearl-harbor-aircraft.asp

Thus my earliest memories were surrounded by the uncertainty of World War II, especially the vulnerability of living on the West coast of the United States. The world was unsettled and families were on the move. Men were drafted and gone. History shows 27,000,000 people moved from the country to big cities in the war years.[8] Jobs changed and expanded as the nation re-industrialized. Women and non-draft age men entered the factory work force en masse. War meant many sacrifices, and many tensions. It meant ration books and saving string and tin foil in balls. It meant shoes that let water in when you walked in the rain. It included those ominous stars in a neighbor's window that a son had been lost in combat. It meant conversion of manufacturing facilities to war machines and munitions.

In reality, the Japanese did attack the West coast, including the Ellwood Oil Field near Santa Barbara (bomb launched from a submarine), Fort Stevens in Astoria as well as firebombs near Brookings, Oregon, launched from floatplanes.[9] Although these attacks created fear and tension, they never amounted to a full-scale invasion.

In addition to world tensions, there was the ever-present tension between my parents. My mother wanted to return to the Pacific Northwest and my father wanted to remain in Southern California, where he had a good job as a longshoreman on the San Pedro docks, not to mention closeness to his two sisters and mother. That tension never ended but became moderated with age and reality. Nonetheless, I grew up thinking Yakima, Washington, my mother's hometown, from which she had migrated to Los Angeles in the 1920s with her two brothers in search of employment, was almost heaven. We should do everything possible to get back there. My Dad said: "I'll only be a fruit picker if we end up in Yakima." We never did, make it to Yakima, that is.

However, fruit pickers we did become. But that was later and only briefly. But some of the best people I know, including a university president, were migrant workers, so it is hardly an indictment.

The dampness of Lomita aggravated my older brother's bronchitis, from which he had suffered since birth in 1930. He has described how Dad would hold him as he coughed himself to sleep every night. Dr. N.,

---

[8] https://books.google.com/books?id=pukbf88n-58C&pg=PA68&lpg=PA68&dq=how+big+was+a+house+in+the+1940s&source=bl&ots=fgsSMVrIjE&sig=KSkkg8FsjteUqm5Fkm6d5QG5eLs&hl=en&sa=X&ved=0CGQQ6AEwDWoVChMIneiqoJm4yAIViFweCh1DfwEC#v=onepage&q=how%20big%20was%20a%20house%20in%20the%201940s&f=false

[9] http://www.history.com/news/history-lists/5-attacks-on-u-s-soil-during-world-war-ii

who delivered my two siblings and me at Torrance General, advised a move to a dry climate, and that meant Yakima to my mother. Dad was willing to move out of California, but not as far as Yakima. And it really was not only Tommy's bronchitis that precipitated the move. Dad suffered from ulcers, which were also diagnosed by Dr. N. These were undoubtedly acerbated by the tension and long hours of working on the waterfront. As it turned out, we were going to leave both the ulcers and the bronchitis in California.

Dad bought a used 1936 Ford truck, red in color with a V-8 engine, crafted by the Ford company only since 1932. [10] It had a flatbed and it was very hot riding in the cab. It took skill to drive that rig, which required double clutching when shifting as well as strong arms to guide the huge tires without the benefit of power steering. We were going to load all of our household goods on that truck and move. I don't recall where. It was just a move. We were part of those 27 million American nomads.

Things were not thrown out in those days. There were no thrift stores like Goodwill [11] and St. Vinnie's [12] for donations. My parents were collectors. Nothing was ever thrown out. Everything we owned was packed onto that truck, including an old Ludwig piano that my parents bought for $50 in 1937. It was a big upright, mahogany in color with real ivory keys, although some were missing. It must have weighed over 400 pounds. My mother played it well and taught both my brother and sister, who were, respectively, nine and six years my senior. Dad had purchased it at $10 a month, payable in "gold coin", according to the contract, until it was free and clear.

I had yet to begin my musical career, but Aunt Mabel, Dad's younger sister, loved to tell the story that when I was two years old, I sat down at the piano, put a book on its music rack and began to play. It probably was more banging than playing. She also observed the music book was upside down. Guess it didn't affect my concert. I always exhibited more style than precision in my musicianship anyway. Everyone in the family, except Dad, learned to play the piano.

Caroline recalls how, at age nine, she was playing the piano when an earthquake hit the region, rocking the piano back and forth and throwing her from the piano bench. Along with the ulcers and bronchitis, this was another reason to move from the Los Angeles area.

---

[10] https://www.thehenryford.org/exhibits/showroom/1932/v8cab.html
[11] https://en.wikipedia.org/wiki/Goodwill_Industries
[12] http://www.svdpusa.org

On the truck was loaded an old refrigerator, which must have had about two cubic feet of storage. There was an ancient wringer-type washing machine, probably a Maytag, plus an overstuffed sofa, well worn, chairs, clothes and just lots of junk. It all went. The fridge kept things lukewarm and the washing machine merely distributed the dirt evenly on the laundry, but it's all we had. All of our stuff was old. There were neither new appliances nor cars during the years of World War II. Every factory was churning out tanks and guns. Cadillac made M-24 light tanks, Maytag, exhaust systems for B-26 bombers, and Chevrolet, T-17 Staghound armored scout cars.[13] Detroit was transitioned into the "Arsenal of Democracy".[14]

Clothes were used until they were worn out, unless they could be discreetly patched. New clothes were simply not available. Although fashion was never a consideration in my family, staying warm, clean and neat were very important. The war created a shortage of natural fabrics, which were used for uniforms, parachutes and other war paraphernalia. But this shortage and war needs promulgated the production of human-made fabrics, such as nylon, which we all enjoyed in later years.[15]

My teachers in grammar school always commented how "clean" we were turned out, even in clothes that were often mended and usually somewhat faded from numerous washings. Our car, clothes and appliances were all old. But so were those of almost everyone we knew.

This was the plan. Dad and Tom, my brother, would drive the Ford V-8, while Mom, driving the 1937 Studebaker Commander, would chauffeur Caroline, my sister, and me. Some Studebakers were labeled "Dictators", meaning they "dictated the automotive standard" but the company re-thought that title in the late 1930's and changed the designation to "Commander". Germany and Italy were both ruled by dictators.[16] In this traveling party there was a two-wheel trailer with a wooden rowboat and Johnson outboard motor that we towed. Dad had crafted that boat and did not want to part with it. We never knew when the earth might be deluged again. I think it was towed behind the Studebaker, which made driving more difficult for my mother.

---

[13] http://www.autonews.com/article/20111031/CHEVY100/310319970/no-new-cars-but-that-didnt-stop-u.s.-automakers-dealers-during-wwii

[14] https://en.wikipedia.org/wiki/Arsenal_of_Democracy

[15] http://digitalscholarship.unlv.edu/cgi/viewcontent.cgi?article=2391&context=thesesdissertations

[16] https://en.wikipedia.org/wiki/Studebaker_Dictator

Where were we going? North appeared to be the destination, depending where Dad could find work. Caroline and I always feared Mom would turn the wrong way in a road and we would be lost. That indeed happened more times than we could remember. Eventually, Tom and Dad would come looking for us and we would be re-united.

Dad always said we were not poor and that we were not like those other people. We were not something reminiscent of a Steinbeck novel.[17] Dad had over $5000 in the bank. Before the depression, he had purchased stock in a building and loan company, which declined drastically in value when the market crashed on October 29, 1929.[18] A few years later, he was offered 10 cents on the dollar to turn the stock in. He refused, at least until 1937, when he bagged 90 cents on the dollar. That accounted for a brand new powder blue Studebaker with an overdrive gear called freewheeling,[19] plus cash in the bank, but never stock again. And he never divested of his bias against building and loan companies.

On the night before leaving California, we had a nice neighborhood send-off, with desserts brought in. It consisted of parishioners from the Calvary Baptist Church where we attended in Lomita. I remember chocolate cake and people standing around talking in the dark, probably because of the Los Angeles war blackouts.[20] There was a young woman in a green coat who kept hugging me, saying good-bye and wishing she could have me. I think I was pretty frightened of the whole thing, fearing my parents might take her up on the proposition. I wanted to go with the family. Grandma and Grandpa Powers, Dad's mother and stepfather, came for a short period. Grandma was sad she was losing her only son for some regions far to the North. As it turned out, we were only going to Oregon, the next state, not Alaska or the Yukon.

Grandma Power's response was strange from a person who had abandoned her children when she divorced in the early 1900's. She kept Aunt Mabel, the youngest, with her, but Dad and Aunt Bernice became street urchins. They were taken by their blacksmith father for a while and then left with foster parents, who treated them well if the boarding fee ware paid, but not so much when the fee was ignored. But years redeem many mistakes and she now had a new husband as well as a son and daughter-in-law, plus three grandchildren on whom she lavished gifts and money on holidays. This family was now going far away and

---

[17] https://www.washingtonpost.com/opinions/75-years-after-the-grapes-of-wrath-we-need-ma-joad-in-the-white-house/2014/04/18/79e8c894-c58b-11e3-bf7a-be01a9b69cf1_story.html
[18] http://www.history.com/topics/1929-stock-market-crash
[19] https://en.wikipedia.org/wiki/Freewheel
[20] https://en.wikipedia.org/wiki/Blackout_(wartime)

there was no texting, mobile phoning nor emailing to stay in contact. She departed the party in her grey Buick coupe among hugs and tears. It would be eleven years before I would see her again. She rarely forgot my birthday in the interim and always referred to me as "Master Pat."

There was no rail line leading out of Lomita, but there was a highway, a narrow two-lane path that would take us north. We began the adventure.

Chapter 2   The Rain in Drain

I don't remember a great deal about the move but we didn't stay in motels, I know that. Motels didn't exist much and they were usually "hot-sheets" cabins. There were no railroads, no freeways, and no interstates, just a series of two-lane roads that took you through every little town as well as some big ones in California. I don't remember the route, either, but I think we stopped near San Francisco to visit Dad's sisters, Aunt Bernice and Uncle Dick, and her family, and possibly Aunt Mabel and Uncle Mel, who lived in Oakland. In route, there were campgrounds where we circled the wagons and built a fire.

Mom cooked on a Coleman stove and it was food items retrieved from a store that very day, probably on our way into the camp. Grocery stores closed at 5 p.m. and were not open on weekends. Shortages were frequent. There was no way to keep food cold the way we traveled, so it was hamburger meatballs with milk and flour gravy almost every night, with white bread dipped into the gravy. We were not conscious of the importance of salads in those days and who could get fresh veggies and fruit on the road. Dessert was rare.

Some of these campgrounds were rough, with people who had much more experience living off the land than we but fewer household goods. The Great Depression was not over for many in the 1940s, in spite of the war machinery that ramped up and put non-service men and many women to work. My Dad was beyond the draft age at 40 and had held a strategic job on the waterfront when war broke out. Dad had been in the Coast Guard in his late teen years for six months, serving on the ice cutter, the USS Bear, " . . . probably the most famous ship in the history of the Coast Guard." [21] But in the 1940's, he only carried a draft card. He was never called to serve during World War II.

Caroline fell in love for the first time in one of these campgrounds, somewhere in Northern California. A cowboy and his young son, Billy N., were camped nearby. Each night, Billy would take out his guitar and sing *Be Honest With Me* to her around the campfire. They would walk and hold hands during the day. Dad soon ended this incipient puppy love by scolding her and telling her she would live in a campground all her life if she got hooked up with likes of this guy. We never learned whether Billy morphed into a famous country-western singer or continued to live in a campground his entire life.

---

[21] https://en.wikipedia.org/wiki/USS_Bear_%281874%29

At times, we lived in these camps for several weeks, waiting for our next round of ration stamps [22] to buy another tankful of gas for two vehicles. All five of us had ration books, required to purchase gas, sugar, and coffee, almost everything. The war was real to all of us, even though it was being fought in theaters east and west, thousands of miles from our shores. There was no CNN immediately to bring a disaster or battle to us. Newsreels in movie theatres, to which we did not go, were the only means of visual news and they were pumped full of propaganda. My father would turn on the radio in the Studebaker for a short time each night for news of the war. We often heard FDR's fireside chats [23] in that manner.

I got in a fight with a local bully, which is pretty remarkable for a three-year old. I think it was over a toy, which was mine, but which this kid wanted. He tried to push me into a dry ditch but Caroline rescued me and sent him on his way with some special expletives. I've fought that battle many times in my life in one-way or another. Bullying is not a new phenomenon. It's gone on for centuries. I've learned in life it can be physical, but more often social and psychological.

One memorable night we were camped near Hornbrook,[24] which is in northern California. There was a train track nearby, going somewhere, and we heard the train whistles. Our site was a small lane off the main road, Highway 99, adjacent to a bridge. We all slept in the Studebaker, Dad in the driver's side with Tom on him, Mom on the other side, with Caroline on her. I slept in the best bunk in the house, atop all the soft goods that were in the backseat, piled almost to the headliner. The state police, shining bright flashlights into the car windows, awakened us around midnight. They advised us to move on as soon as possible in the morning. Bridges were vulnerable to bombing and terrorism, not by enemy planes, but by native sympathizers. That's why innocent Japanese-Americans [25] were interred and no American admitted they spoke German. We stayed the night, a bit nervously, and moved on the next morning, discombobulated, but compliant. So forewarned, we never camped near bridges again.

The police were nice, though. They probably routed a caravan each night from this pristine spot on the Klamath River. Police were not to be feared in those days and they really were concerned with our safety, more than observing the letter of the law.

---

[22] http://www.ameshistory.org/exhibits/events/rationing.htm
[23] http://www.history.com/topics/fireside-chats
[24] http://www.city-data.com/city/Hornbrook-California.html
[25] http://www.ushistory.org/us/51e.asp

I don't recall how long it took us to arrive in Oregon or even why Oregon was chosen. It wasn't Yakima, but my mother's radar said it was a lot closer than Lomita. We spent time in a Springfield, Oregon campground. Again, it was rough and kids were mean-spirited. In the 1940s, campgrounds were dirt fields where you could pitch a tent. There were no pools, no bathhouses. I have no idea how we kept clean, but my mother carried Lifebuoy and Oxydol [26] like armor and they were used on our bodies and their coverings. Sometimes we used a hose with cold water when no one was looking. My brother and sister undoubtedly took delight in hosing me down. Other times, water was heated in a pan on the Coleman stove and we were told to wash in "two places". I was always the last to get the water, so it was rarely hot.

Tom and Caroline often ganged up on me when Mom was not around, then would be so sorry for what they had done. I lived through it, however. Like most siblings, there was a healthy dose of baiting and teasing, but also a protective side that kept me from being hurt.

Daily bathing was not considered necessary in those days, as long as one had a PTA[27] bath between. If there had been a facility for washing clothes, undoubtedly my mother would have slaved over it for hours to produce clean clothes for us. She always believed cleanliness is next to Godliness, but I'm not certain it says that in the scriptures. But it could explain all the foot washing in the Bible.

My brother and sister were enrolled for three weeks in a Springfield school, Caroline in the fourth grade and Tom in the seventh. Springfield had a population of less than 4,000 (compared to over 60,000 now),[28] so it was a small town by most standards. Dad scouted the area and even looked for real estate to purchase. Never had the family owned a house. We had always been renters. He located a 160-acre sheep ranch in Drain, Oregon, population 597.[29] We swelled the census to 602.

It had a real house with a bathroom, an unfinished attic, a large barn with livestock, including an old horse named Silver. There were two cows, Tiny and Betty, which became pets. We would be farmers, raising hay, harvesting some of the timber, and becoming glued-down residents. The price of the farm was $5500 and Dad took a mortgage, something he had never done before and would never do again. It was a bargain because the average price of a house alone was $6950 in those days.

---

[26] http://www.cleanlink.com/sm/article/1940s-Cleaning-During-And-After-World-War-II--15618
[27] http://www.urbandictionary.com/define.php?term=PTA+bath
[28] https://en.wikipedia.org/wiki/Springfield,_Oregon
[29] https://en.wikipedia.org/wiki/Drain,_Oregon

The house was big and comfortable by 1940's standards. No furnace, so heat came from a circulating stove in the living room plus a kitchen wood stove, which heated water through coils connected to a water tank. We had to light a kitchen fire to get a warm bath but who didn't in those days.

One of my chores was carrying kindling and wood for the kitchen fire, but I doubt I was the sole supplier at age three. Using the axe was forbidden. It was undoubtedly the family work ethic that required every member to do chores to contribute to the family welfare.

Elk Creek, that dumps into the Umpqua River, which then becomes a mighty river near Winchester Bay, after the Smith River at Reedsport joins it, ran through our property. As we observed, it was just a small stream, or so it seemed. We had to cross Elk Creek to get to all of the property. There was a swinging bridge and a hand-operated trolley for crossing near the house. Our sheep were all on the other side. There was an access road for cars further down stream, which worked well when the creek was low, usually in the summer.

My siblings, who were basically city kids, quickly adapted to farm life, helping with the chores, like milking the cows, and retrieving eggs from the hen house. My sister was a champion milkmaid. I sometimes got to help feed the chickens by throwing out grain, but was afraid of aggressive chickens, which would try to peck my legs.

After camping in small spaces, we had a big farmhouse to play in. My brother and sister would really scare me by putting empty cardboard boxes over me. That may have been what made me so afraid of the dark in my early years and convinced me I wanted to be cremated when I pass on, not buried. It was all good fun and meant in a jovial way, but when two older kids gang up on you, it was good Mom was there to protect me. I certainly became a "momma's boy".

There were happy times in Drain with a family that lived close by, the Ks. George K. had worked on the waterfront with Dad. We would have picnics with them and hike or drive into the mountains back of our house, which rose like huge anthills. The kids would ride Silver, the horse. The K.s had a daughter named Ruth about Tom's age and she had a crush on him. She was plump and cute but it was probably just puppy love, with some groping and kissing. My brother always had a high amount of testosterone and attracted girls. In his heyday, it was allegedly more than groping and kissing.

We lived two miles from the school, [30] which still is used in Drain. There was a school bus. My sister was always running for it, since her hair was braided every morning. Never a morning person, anyway, Dad and Tom would egg her on with: "The school bus is waiting for you". She went into a panic and I can remember her running down the long driveway many mornings, not quite ready, not quite braided, for public appearance but determined to get on that bus. If you did not, you walked. Fortunately, her homeroom teacher would finish the braiding task.

And walking my brother did. He wanted to join the basketball team, which practiced after school. There was no activity bus. That meant hiking home in the dark down Highway 38, high and spooky trees on both sides of the road with things ready to jump out at you at every turn. The bigger danger during the day was log trucks, but those didn't run at night. Dad said Tom would need to walk home if he wanted to participate.

The first night after practice, Tom started down those two miles from Drain to the farm, scared out of his mind as a seventh grader. It got darker and darker the further he went. But he looked down the road and saw a small flickering light, which grew brighter the faster he walked toward it. Dad had lit the kerosene lantern and was coming down the road to meet him, protecting his firstborn in spite of all the gruffness that went with it. Dad did that for me, too, in Mosier when the bus returned late after an "away" game in Eastern Oregon and I had to walk home past a raucous beer hall late at night.

We went to an auction in Cottage Grove, probably either to buy or sell farm equipment. It was cold and rainy. We had no food but Dad scouted the surroundings and came back with hamburgers for all, the first time I had ever tasted such a delicacy. I'm still a Whooper fan. The auctioneer was glib and fast, as they can be, and when an upright piano was brought to the stage, he asked if anyone in the crowd could demonstrate it. Dad shouted out his daughter could. Caroline, age ten, bounced onto the stage, ever the ready entertainer if there were an audience, and rolled out a spirited rendition of *You're A Grand Old Flag*. [31] It was her own arrangement, classical technique but mostly rag.

The piano sold after the bids were run up to a good price and the auctioneer pressed a 50-cent piece into Caroline's hand, her first professional gig. She already had a way with an audience and still seeks

---

[30] http://www.cityofdrain.org/Community/Schools/tabid/4129/language/en-US/Default.aspx
[31] https://en.wikipedia.org/wiki/You%27re_a_Grand_Old_Flag

the affirmation through music that she is okay, even now, at age 82. Insecurities are hard to lose when you're practically born with them. I know that well too. You can never be good enough, kind enough, good-looking enough, loved enough, Christian enough, clean enough, have white teeth enough, rich enough or, for my family, talented enough.

We did not remain at Drain long, probably less than a year but over a summer, because Caroline and Tom moved to the next grade, she, fifth, and he, eighth. There would be more moves for these grades. The land was not productive and Dad could not draw a living from it. The timber was not worth the effort and growing hay only produced enough for our livestock. We had a young bull named Brownie that became a pet during this time. He was docile around Dad but terrorized the rest of us should we wander into his path. I was never one who wanted to participate in Pamplona [32] marathons, whether in Spain or Drain.

Since help was scarce on the San Pedro waterfront, Dad returned to Southern California in the spring to earn some fast money. Grandpa Powers ran a gang there and knew his stepson was a good stevedore. Public transportation was sketchy, so bus and train travel were not possible. The military had priority. Buses were packed with soldiers, many standing or sitting on duffle bags in the aisles to reach their destination.

Dad hitchhiked to San Pedro. This was common during World War II. There were fewer vehicles on the road and a greater trust of strangers. In 1940, there were 245 cars per 1000 people, even fewer in 1945, or about 3 million cars. (There are currently 253,000,000 cars in U.S. now, slightly over 400 per 1000 people.) [33] In those days, there were not many cars on the road leading to Los Angeles but there were trucks. Dad was usually lucky in getting picked up by a long-truck hauler, who needed the company, and may have even traded off driving because my father could handle big equipment.

Where was that railroad to somewhere when we needed it? It did not run through our property, anyway, but rather, from Roseburg, through Drain, to Reedsport. The rail line along Highway 38 had been built in the early 1900s to move the harvested lumber to market as well as for passenger travel between inland and the coast.

---

[32] http://www.red2000.com/spain/pamplona/
[33] http://knoema.com/atlas/United-States-of-America/Passenger-cars-per-1000-people

I don't know the time of year, but it was probably in the spring, when rain is heavy in the foothills of the Oregon coastal range. Drain receives in excess of 50 inches of rain a year, much of it coming November through March.[34] The small creek behind our house swelled to flood proportions, since it probably was one of those years when there was seven inches of rain in a single day. Debris and dead trees came down the creek, taking out the swinging bridge and trolley in short order. Our nearest foot route was cut-off and our livestock were stranded without food. My mother panicked, probably burst into tears but then we got help from neighbors to deliver hay to our livestock. The flood subsided, leaving the dirt driveway from the house to Highway 38 covered with water. Dad returned soon after. Since our front area was still flooded, he used his little rowboat to deliver my siblings to the bus stop.

I don't know how my mother endured without my father in the house, but she did. Her great Christian faith carried her through, but imagine a 30-something wife with three kids, all under 15, running a farm and weathering flood conditions. There was probably little money in her purse either. However, she had the power of prayer. Her only communication with Dad was snail-mail, which meant a small white envelope with a three-cent stamp on it. She drove, but never comfortably.

What groceries we had came from the barnyard, chicken house or the store of preserved fruit and garden vegetables she faithfully canned each autumn. But I never felt deprivation because we did not have food. There always seemed to be plenty, even if somewhat monotonous, and I was well fed or even over fed. I was not a chubby child, but definitely a mesomorph,[35] who would be considered and teased as fat later in school. There were no chef-inspired television shows delighting viewers with tasty concoctions, so we never missed what we did not know or have. We were just learning about Betty Crocker [36] but had never heard of Julia Child.[37]

I developed my life-long fear of snakes at Drain. A huge serpent came into our yard while Dad was absent. It was probably only four-feet long but in my mind as well as with Mom we saw it as a ten-foot boa constrictor. It terrified my mother and she was certain it was a diamond-backed rattler. It was probably just a big garter snake, helpful to nature in reducing the rodent population. In spite of her terror, she went after that snake with a vengeful shovel and beat it into a coma,

---

[34] http://www.bestplaces.net/climate/city/oregon/drain
[35] http://www.britannica.com/science/mesomorph
[36] http://www.bettycrocker.com
[37] http://www.pbs.org/food/chefs/julia-child/

since Caroline and Tom were in school She was convinced it was Satan. She subsequently buried it in a shallow grave, but it soon exhumed itself after it awoke, rising mid-body from the dirt, just about the time the school bus delivered my siblings home.

I don't remember the denouement of this incident, but I think my brave brother did it in by using the shovel to make it more than one snake. It stayed buried and its relatives knew better than to return, since they had been advised we lived by the motto on the Gadsden flag, *"Don't tread on me!"* [38] Snakes have raised my blood pressure ever since, whether viewing a picture or video. Yet I have stepped over them in the desert and placed my hands and feet where I could have been struck. I even recently went to the emergency room in Tucson with a suspected snakebite from walking at night. The doctor said we would never know for certain, but it must have been a dry bite since I had no affects from any venom. My snake phobia is a strange fear, evoked by memory and pictures more than actually meeting one in the wild.

To their great credit, Caroline and Tom were very mature in their responsibilities, which included feeding and milking the cows, tending Silver, mucking the manure from the barn and gathering the eggs. Household and barnyard chores were neither reminded nor rewarded, other than verbally. They were just done without grumbling and without money because you were part of the family. My sister tended me much of the time, because Mom was either pitching hay or manure, if not washing, cleaning or cooking. If I were outside, I was usually at the edge of the action, watching, possibly helping or getting in the way, but more likely carrying a cat or a chick, which I had befriended. Some of my best friends have always been domestic animals, or, as we say now, companion animals. Their love was always unconditional.

By the time Dad returned from Los Angeles, it had been decided to sell the farm and move on. Mom said the place should have been called *Rain* (I think W. Somerset Maugham had already coined that title),[39] not *Drain*. Dad sold the place for the same as he paid, $5500, and we moved on. He was no longer mortgaged and to be debt free was important to him, a lesson he passed on to his children. However, we did not necessarily heed this advice in equal measure, given the advantage of secured debt as an investment opportunity in our tax laws. This time our move included two cows, Tiny and Betty, an array of caged Rhode Island Red chickens and Brownie, who had morphed into a steer. The little rowboat and Silver, the resident horse, were left for the new farm owners, the

---

[38] https://en.wikipedia.org/wiki/Gadsden_flag
[39] https://csrags.wordpress.com/2015/05/01/somerset-maughams-rain/

former to ford the creek, the latter to ride the range.   Next stop: Yoncalla, by auto and truck, not train. The railroad did not run there.

Chapter 3   Rustic Setting In Yoncalla

Yoncalla,[40] Oregon, is not far from Drain. I'll never know how Dad made his contacts to get jobs or to find houses, but he always did. Early in my remembrance, he was charming to strangers who treated him right, brusque and rude to those who did not. The family got both sides of Dad from time to time and his mood could change without any warning. You always could tell when to scatter by looking at his eyes.

However he did it, Dad located an old two-story country house and farm outside Yoncalla in Scott's Valley. He was ever the provider for his family. It was a homestead that needed a tenant farmer. We moved in. We were responsible for caring for the livestock, particularly a herd of sheep that roamed the area, in exchange for rent and perhaps a small stipend. There were turkeys to tend as well. Since turkeys are not the brightest of fowl, their young were frequently killed by chicken hawks. When they roosted at night, they often crowded together and consequently smothered. They only way to prevent this was to go into their coop late in the evening and separate them.

There was also a resident horse, Molly, who was too fat to saddle. Tom and Caroline rode her bareback, their legs sticking out 90 degrees from her generous body. Molly was somewhat flatulent and farted rhythmically in cadence as she was ridden, which provided much entertainment for all of us.

 Dr. T., a retired physician owned this fiefdom and we became his serfs for a short period of time. It was wagged by local gossips that this doctor had performed abortions in his practice and still did, for those who needed this drastic form of birth control. No one used the word "abortion" and there was no whisper of this practice in polite circles, but somehow, everyone in town knew.

I did not know what an abortion was nor how it occurred or by whom, why and where. Later I learned my aunt's sister, my mother confided to me, had had one because she preferred not to be a mother. Strangely, however, she was another one of those women who wanted to adopt me, once I was out of diapers and was a toddler, not a baby.

If Drain were wet, Scott's Valley was wetter, if that is possible. All I can remember is that it rained all the time. I was always outside playing in the rain and I was always wet. The ground was soaked and Molly, the resident horse, fell on her back in a mud hole. A big tractor had to be brought in to extricate the beast from her watery domain. The sheep

---

[40] https://en.wikipedia.org/wiki/Yoncalla,_Oregon

suffered from some disease [41] or blight that made them sick enough to die. Several did. Their coats did not grow into fine wool for shearing. The turkey herd was decimated by chicken hawks and questionable roosting practices. The doctor was upset that we were not caring for the animals and made threatening overtures and statements about our tenancy. He was severe but my dad could be as well. It was not a good situation. Dad worked in one of the local sawmills, too, as he had done in Drain, so sheep herding was only a part-time endeavor for him. We needed the money so as not to dip into that $5000 savings, which was earning less than 2% per annum in the First National Bank.

Dad held the pocketbook and we never knew how much was in it. Mom did not either, since he paid for family groceries by going shopping with her. She had no pocket money. While they had lived in California when first married in 1928 and until our departure in 1942, she took the paycheck and managed the family money. This way, she could conserve on groceries and buy something for the house, like curtains, napkins or tablecloths.

Somewhat as retribution for forcing a move to the Northwest or some other reason, Dad withdrew this privilege and kept tight strings on all funds. Retribution may be too strong a word, in spite of the Los Angeles versus Yakima tug-of-war between them. This arrangement may have been simply fear of running out of money. It could also have been his desire for us not to know how little we really had. Dad always felt Mom was not a good manager of money, but it was probably more perception than reality. Typically, though, if Mom had $20, a dollar would be sent to each of twenty charities or churches.

In December of that year, we were in Scott's Valley. On Christmas morning, I remember looking through the grate that allowed hot air to ascend from the huge South Bend [42] wood-burning stove in the kitchen. The tree was up and there were presents under it. It must have been a surprise to all of us children. Money must have come in or a decision had been made to spend some of it. The upstairs was warm from a hearty fire built with fir and cedar downstairs and we were ready for Christmas. Presents were never opened on Christmas Eve, regardless of the pleas of us three kids, only Christmas morning. This would occur only after we had done morning ablutions, eaten an extra-large bowl of Cream of Wheat and had evacuated, which, in Scott's Valley, meant making an outside trip to the two-holed privy about 200 feet from the house in the rain.

41

http://ag.ansc.purdue.edu/sheep/ansc442/Semprojs/2007/hoofcare/hoofcare.htm
42 http://www.antiquestoves.com/south.htm

After presents, the rooster who had accompanied us from Drain, graced our Christmas table with mashed potatoes and cranberries plus steam pudding [43] with hard sauce for dessert. Steam pudding was a delicacy, made faithfully from Grandma Power's recipe and only lacking here what Grandma would have added, a generous portion of quality brandy. Liquor was never in our home in those years, not because of belief but, rather, parsimony. It was a memorable Christmas morning. Not all holidays were like this one.

I had pet animals in that brief time and each had a name. We had visitors one rainy afternoon. I scurried to retrieve my pet chicken, which was actually a teenage pullet. I ran to their car to show them my beautiful pet only to have my brother point to my jacket once I arrived on the scene. It was covered with juicy chicken poop from a bird that preferred feathered companions to human. I was embarrassed and later unrelentingly teased for this social gaffe.

Incidentally, this same thing happened to me later in life, when I greeted guests in our retirement community home, holding our newly arrived miniature pinscher, Benson, which had just shat on my white designer polo shirt. That polo was never the same but the pet was well worth it, in both cases.

In the spring, quite surreptitiously, we packed our goods in the truck, which was hidden in the big barn. We loaded the car, slept in the hay in the barn until midnight and departed Yoncalla in the darkness of night. I remember being awakened and led to the car. We exited this domain without headlights until we got to Highway 99 [44] heading south. We never saw Yoncalla, Scott's Valley or Drain again for some time. We were on our way back to Southern California and the waterfront. But we never made it. At least Yakima was out of the picture. And the population of Yoncalla continued to be held in check by the good doctor.

---

[43] http://www.bbcgoodfood.com/technique/how-steam-pudding
[44] http://www.aaroads.com/guide.php?page=s0099or

Chapter 4   Shampoo With the Crews

Mother had friends from her early years in Bend, Oregon, where her father, an itinerate carpenter, homesteaded a half-section, [45] 320 acres, and built a house. Her mother was a hard working Hungarian immigrant, from the twin towns of Buda and Pest, who married John Hazelbaum, a German immigrant from Breslau. Census records of their arrival in America were lost, but they apparently came through Ellis Island [46] around the turn of the 20th Century. Their skill in English was minimal and the name Hazuka was written down, corrupted from what it had been, Hazelbaum. This might have been from verbal misunderstanding or simply poor spelling in America's language.

It's possible John Hazelbaum, now John Hazuka, was Jewish and was escaping a bad situation in Germany, whether pogram [47] or poverty. It was never learned whether they were married before their arrival or after, or even married at all. But her father, a Free Mason and spiritualist, [48] was always home long enough to impregnate his wife and then leave her while he was off to the next woodworking job, or, as we often speculated, another family. Mom's mom bore three children and said enough was enough. The rest of the pregnancies she took care of in a way known only to her, but it did involve knitting needles or clothes hangers. It eventually killed her. She had to work to support her family and the family was big enough with three kids: Mom and two older brothers, Rudy and Julius.

The Crews had been neighbors and friends to the Hazukas in Bend, Mr. and Mrs. Crew, plus three kids, Emma, Bill and Kitty. When the Hazuka's Bend house burned, the homestead was abandoned and the family moved to Yakima. Thus the romance with the Yakima fruit-growing region began and manifest destiny was returning there for my mother.

I do not know how or why we contacted the Crews, now in Northern California. It must have been with a simple letter and a simple written response. We must have needed a place to camp until a permanent destination could be determined. Somehow we ended up in the mountains of Northern California near Magalia [49] in a small village called

---

[45] http://thelawdictionary.org/section-of-land/
[46] http://www.history.com/topics/ellis-island
[47] http://www.thefreedictionary.com/Pogram
[48] http://www.thefreedictionary.com/Spiritualist
[49] http://www.ontheridge.com/magalia.html

De Sabla, which is in Butte County.[50] The closest city now is Chico, the closest town, Paradise.

The arrangement was a series of guest cabins and we took two. We must have paid rent or had an arrangement for payment to the Crews. The cabins were old and rustic. The floors were wood planks laid on dirt, with openings that allowed rodents and insects, particularly ants, to enter. Dust was everywhere. My mother did her usual cleaning, broom and rags in hand, with Bon Ami and Purex and we moved in. There was no running water, unless you count the flume across the road. There was a privy with a Montgomery Ward catalog for morning evacuations and midday meditations.

Bill Crew was a rugged outdoorsman, who carried a Springfield 30.6. He and Dad were simpatico. Bill worked for the local utility company as a ditch (flume) walker. He had about 20 miles of flume to maintain. Dad was soon hired to work on the same lines. It was rugged country, replete with diamond-backed rattlesnakes, deer and black bear. We were told to be extra careful wherever we stepped to avoid snakebite.

We also knew that this guarded warning was to keep us out of their local goldmine, which Bill claimed was resplendent with nuggets. He still panned for gold and we were shown some of his nuggets. The Crew's gold mine had collapsed inward and needed to be dug out and shored with timber beams. They were very protective of this mine. This region of California was known for its gold. It was near Magalia that A.K. Stearns, a local worker, found a gold nugget in 1859, which weighed 54 lbs., [51] so there was gold in "them thar hills."

Gold was not of particular interest to us. Shelter was. But the Crews were always suspicious that we were somehow after their gold, even though they had not quite located that bountiful vein that would reward them with huge nuggets.

Emma was Bill's spinster sister and she had been a Gibson girl beauty [52] in her youth, but was now faded and gaunt. She never allowed sun on her face and I have no recollection of her face or essence, only a figure that was Emma, tall and thin. Emma had beautiful clothes but they were all of an earlier generation. She was polite and kind, sharing canned bear and deer meat with us on occasion, saying it was a special type of beef. The bear meat was very greasy and the deer meat wild tasting.

---

[50] https://en.wikipedia.org/wiki/DeSabla,_California
[51] http://www.ghosttowns.com/states/ca/magalia.html
[52] http://www.eyewitnesstohistory.com/gibson.htm

By contrast, Kitty Fox, Emma and Bill's other sibling, was older and had gone and done. She was wild and free. She was apparently divorced and she would often say to her sister: "It is better to have loved and lost than never to have loved at all." It was not an original thought, however, but, rather, a line penned by Alfred Lord Tennyson.[53] But it was Kitty Fox.

She took me, about four years of age, under her wing. I helped her pick up dry cow piles, which she used in the stove and for garden fertilizer. I thought it was as delightful as harvesting strawberries. My brother, sister and Dad would tease me about the two of us in a field, butts to the wind, picking up cow turds like gold nuggets. There were undoubtedly more of these nuggets than the true ones anyway. And they didn't weight 54 lbs.

One day I was playing outside around an old abandoned kitchen stove. I opened the lid on the stove with a poker and heard a funny rattle. It frightened me and I ran and told Bill and Dad. They laughed and said it was nothing: "Just be careful." A few days later, Bill brought a sealed can to the front of one of our cabins, opened it at a distance and an enormous snake crawled out, spitting mad at confinement. Bill teased it so we could hear it rattle again and again. It was a timber rattler (Northern Pacific rattlesnake,) [54] brown-green in color with a wonderful reticulation on its backside and ten rattles. Exercise done, Bill took his Smith and Wesson revolver and sent the serpent to eternity. No one ever said there was a snake in the stove, but I think I had escaped a great danger.

Tom and Caroline had been yanked out of school mid-year in Yoncalla and entered De Sabla School once we were settled. It was a one-room school. Miss W. was the lone teacher. Tom was the only student in his grade, as was Caroline. They had to walk five-miles each day to get to the school, but locals, who knew everyone, including log truck drivers, usually picked them up. Caroline recalls it was a good experience and the teacher was highly competent. A morning task for the boys was building the wood stove in the school. It apparently was never a chore and done with joy and enthusiasm. At his eighth-grade graduation, Tom sang the *Star-Spangled Banner* while Caroline accompanied him on the piano.

As the baby of the family, I had to go to bed earlier than my siblings. They frolicked in the twilight, playing "kick the can", as I entered dreamland in one of our cabins. One particular night I had a detailed

---

[53] http://www.brainyquote.com/quotes/quotes/a/alfredlord153702.html
[54] https://www.wildlife.ca.gov/News/Snake

dream that Adolph Hitler [55] had marched up the hill to our cabin with a huge army and kidnaped me. It was all so vivid and I knew exactly what he looked like, undoubtedly from pictures in a *Life Magazine* I had seen somewhere. I woke and saw a portrait of Franklin Delano Roosevelt, hanging on the wall of our cabin. I then felt safe. It was our picture and not at all to Bill Crew's liking. He always said he was going to blow it away with his pistol, much like he had done with the rattlesnake. Incidentally, we pronounced our President's name as it is now and should have been. It was always "Rose-a-velt", never "Ruh-sa-velt." [56]

We stayed the summer in the mountains of Northern California, where it got hot and muggy always with an omnipresent fear of forest fires. The relationship with the Crews was tenuous, and it was probably due to something like rent owed and not paid, or some misunderstanding of our tenancy in their woods. Perhaps we had overstayed our welcome, even for long-lasting friends from Bend. Perhaps they thought we were after their gold.

We all did excursions in the higher mountains for beehives, from which we extricated the hive with fire on the end of a stick, so we could retrieve their bounty of honey. This was usually accompanied by a generous array of picnic food, because Emma and Kitty were great gardeners and Bill always had fresh meat, in season or not.

One hot summer day, we three kids diverted the flume before it reached the Crew's house. Mom washed clothes and we played under the cool water in bathing suits, relishing the day with abandon. The party soon ended, though, when Kitty, shampoo covering her long artic blond hair, came running up the road to see why their water had ceased. Playtime was soon over so Kitty could rinse. We moved soon after. The train kept moving.

On our way to the next place, somewhere in Northern California, we pulled alongside a park in Chico, which had a school across the street. An alert teacher saw a teachable moment and brought her entire classroom to see the cattle. Dad was a teaching tool for her, demonstrating how to milk a cow in a trailer. We looked like the proverbial *Grapes of Wrath* to these city kids but I don't think anyone was embarrassed by the chance encounter. People were people and not status conscious in the war years. We were all fighting the same war with a common enemy. City kids in those days probably thought milk came from a bottle. It doesn't, of course. It comes from plastic gallon jugs.

---

[55] http://www.biography.com/people/adolf-hitler-9340144
[56] http://www.theodoreroosveltcenter.org/Blog/2013/January/21-How-do-you-pronounce-Roosevelt.aspx

Somewhere on this trip, we camped where a farmer needed workers to pick tomatoes. It was a chance to earn money, so we stayed a few days. I guess that qualified us for the appellation "migrant workers". I helped a little but mostly I played in the grass while the family worked. Tom and Caroline earned enough to spring for a used bicycle at our next home. The bike, which I eventually inherited, was a disaster from the get-go. It was assembled from a variety of components from assorted bikes. Nothing ever interfaced precisely. Nonetheless, it was a bike, with pedals, wheels and a coaster brake. It was certainly not the Schwinn Continental, glamorized by film stars like Ronald Reagan and Jane Wyman in brochures, [57] but it was a bike that could carry two kids to school. Caroline would ride on the handlebars while Tom pedaled. There was no shift and no derailleur. Bike production, like cars and appliances, was curtailed between 1942-45 for the war effort. This was the best they could find. It transported them to school at our next stop, which was Talent, Oregon.[58]

---

[57] http://waterfordbikes.com/SchwinnCat/flschwinn_1941_1950/1946b_04.html
[58] http://www.cityoftalent.org

Chapter 5   Too Much Talent

Talent, close to Ashland, is barely over the Oregon border from California. Why did we end up here? I have no idea. I just went along with all these moves, thinking it was the way everyone lived. At my age, what choice did I have? As hard as it was on my parents, nomadic journeys were now a lifestyle. I was almost five years old and school was on my horizon. I was assured school would be a good experience for me, as I saw my sister off to the sixth grade and my brother to the ninth at Talent High School.

Talent was a good time in our life. We bought the little house we lived in. Dad worked in a mill and Mom was a homemaker in a small house, sans indoor bathroom, but at least with running water. It was five acres and we had our cows, chickens and possibly pigs by now. We were well fed and so were the livestock. Alfalfa grew on the five acres. Southern Oregon continues to be a unique area, even now, with the arts emphasis in Ashland and the beauty of the Rogue River.

I have always loved Ashland, from the Lithia water in the park to the Varsity movie theatre across the street, where we saw *Three Caballeros*, an animated Disney flick, [59] to the shouts of the migrant Mexicans in the theatre and their "¡Viva México!" when their *bandera* (flag) was flashed on the screen. Mexicans were guest workers who came legally to our country to work the crops. We enjoyed hearing their musical language bantered about. I'm still not competent in Spanish but I am planning on fluency in heaven, with perhaps some ability in French and German as well.

There must have been money here because both my siblings were in the school band. Tom played string bass and Caroline, cymbals. They were both very musical. This was a real perk in a school curriculum before music education was a common offering.

The house was small and tidy on a secondary road near Highway 99 at the end of the pasture. If Dad did not work in a mill, he probably was a foreman or a go-to for one of the local ranchers because he had so many practical skills. He could handle most machines, whether trucks, tractors, combines or threshers. He could coax them into starting and minding their manners, even if it required an oil or filter change.

Dad had a wonderful visual-spatial intelligence [60] that he never imparted to me, although Tom got a great deal of it. He could look at a distance,

---

[59] http://disney.wikia.com/wiki/The_Three_Caballeros
[60] http://www.tecweb.org/styles/gardner.html

whether height, width or length and measure it in his mind, never being off by a few inches or more. In a sawmill, he could look at a log and tell the board feet it would produce. Similarly in a mill yard, he could look at several stacks of lumber and mentally calculate how much would be needed to build a house. Dad could plant, fertilize and harvest crops, bale hay and store it in a barn, which he had built. He could butcher a calf, pig, turkey or chicken. He could transform a bull into a steer. He was a skilled cat skinner, [61] learned in the fields of Knights Landing when he was 13 years old.

He could break the bead on a flat tire manually, take it off its rim, vulcanize the puncture, replace tube and tire, pump it full of air, remount the tire and put it back on the vehicle, whether bike, car or truck, before you could say AAA. He could fit new rings on the pistons in an old engine, grind the valves, replace the camshaft and adjust the timing with a timing light, one hand behind him. He knew tools and never had to search for the right socket. His eye told him what to use. He was a born problem solver, using the tools and material he had in front of him, if only baling wire. He could make do. Had he lived in medieval times, he would have slain dragons.

He was strong, muscular and wiry, with big shoulders and a thick chest. He stood 5'10" in his prime, although it was more like 5'2" when he passed at 98, in 1999. He wanted to live into the new millennium so his tombstone would say 1901-2000, but missed it by 40 days. My Dad was real, never easy, never predictable, but a real person. He was a hard worker and a wonderful provider for his family.

His complexion was light, his hair Irish red, with freckles and skin sensitive to sun exposure. I got that as well as the predilection to skin cancer, even if I didn't get the spatial intelligence. If he had to work eight hours, he probably gave more than ten hours of labor to his employer. Most recognized his work ethic and great honesty. He was almost never without employment and he usually ended up in charge of a gang, crew, system or a process. Had he gone to college, he undoubtedly would have designed bridges, dams, if not pyramids and skyscrapers. He was incredibly intelligent, quick, a wiz with numbers and his Parker Penmanship, [62] even in his tenth decade of life, was flawless. Nonetheless, he never finished the eighth grade because he had to earn a living. There were rough edges, for certain, but emotion never got in the way of doing what he was paid to do. He never called in sick to work. He never failed the family. He never cheated on Mom.

---

[61] http://dictionary.reference.com/browse/catskinner
[62] https://en.wikipedia.org/wiki/Palmer_Method

When he worked on the non-unionized docks in San Pedro, early in his marriage, so reported Mom, he would pull 36-hour shifts, come home covered with dust and grime and fall asleep in the bathtub. She had to check on him so he did not drown. Before unionization on the waterfront, unemployed men looked down the hold of the ship being loaded, waiting for someone to drop from fatigue so they could have their job. It got better after the unions were established in 1935, [63] but Dad participated in some violent strikes, so he said, where scabs [64] were beaten and chased from the docks. He was always a union man and carried his ILA (International Lonshoremen's Association) union card with great pride.

Much like Drain, in Talent Dad hitched a ride to San Pedro to work on the docks for six weeks, leaving Mom in charge of five acres, two cows, a heifer, several chickens and three kids. Again, I'm not certain how she managed but I remember that the heifer got into the alfalfa field one evening, ate too much, bloated and died. How glad Mom was when she saw a freight truck drop a hitchhiker off the main road. She ran across the field to embrace Dad. That was the greatest show of affection I ever observed between my parents. They probably had good sex that night. I'm sure my siblings were listening because the house was very small.

I tried to learn to tell time at Talent. This was part of being a "big boy". It was "if the big hand is on and the little hand is on . . ." sort of thing. I didn't want to go through this process. I wanted a Gestalt [65] and to just be able to do it. I'd look at that Big Ben, which had survived our peregrinations, and would try to decipher what time it was in terms of where we were in the passage of the day. I usually got it backwards, 3 p.m. becoming a quarter past noon and 9 a.m. becoming quarter to twelve. Was it half past noon or 6 p.m.? I never missed on high noon however. How much easier with a digital clock but it has been said today's kids can't tell time from an analog timepiece, much like my issues in 1945. We know millennials have a problem using a dial telephone and young children try to zoom in on pictures in paper books as if they were using an iPad. Sometimes I think we're not better now, just different. Every generation has probably observed that as they were replaced by the next.

My mother listened to soaps on the radio. *The Guiding Light* [66] was a favorite. We also listened to the hit parade once a week. My favorite was

---

[63] https://en.wikipedia.org/wiki/International_Longshoremen%27s_Association
[64] http://www.urbandictionary.com/define.php?term=scab
[65] http://www.vocabulary.com/dictionary/gestalt
[66] https://www.otrcat.com/soap-operas-during-the-golden-age-of-radio

Al Dexter's version of *Pistol Packing Mama*.[67] I could sing it by heart and pouted when it was toppled from first place. I heard my mother crooning *Oh, What a Beautiful Morning* while she was hanging freshly washed clothes out-of-doors one morning. *Oklahoma!,*[68] the Rodgers and Hammerstein blockbuster, had premiered on Broadway in 1943. Its music had invaded the people's culture.

There was a daily newspaper, delivered each evening. We kids would check out the "funnies" to catch the adventures of Smilin' Jack,[69] Terry and the Pirates [70] or Buz Sawyer.[71] Dad would read the newspaper each night, often commenting about something that was going on in the world.

It was 1945 and many thought the war would end soon. Little did we know that the European powers, anticipating a post-World War II world, had begun the process of dividing Europe at the Yalta conference [72] in February.

I was in the back yard of the Talent house when the news was received that FDR had died in Warm Springs, Georgia, on April 12 [73] and Harry S. Truman was now President. The only President I had ever known was Roosevelt and this was traumatic for me. My mother cried, because she and Dad were staunch Democrats who believed FDR not only brought us out of the Great Depression, but also gave us the safety net of Social Security in 1935. Since then, I have survived twelve additional Presidents and the union has held.

Ed Clark's photo from *Life Magazine* [74] of Chief Petty Officer (USN) Graham W. Jackson playing his piano-accordion at the news of Roosevelt's passing was well imprinted in my memory at age five. I still have a copy of that picture on my computer. It says so much and conveys so much grief, not only of one man, but also of the entire nation. Love or hate a President, you always grieve at their passing.

---

[67] http://txmusic.com/texas-treasures/story-behind-the-song-pistol-packin-mama
[68] http://www.playbillvault.com/Show/Detail/4221/Oklahoma
[69] https://en.wikipedia.org/wiki/The_Adventures_of_Smilin%27_Jack
[70] .wikipedia.org/wiki/Terry_and_the_Pirates_(comic_strip)
[71] https://en.wikipedia.org/wiki/Buz_Sawyer
[72] https://history.state.gov/milestones/1937-1945/yalta-conf
[73] http://www.eyewitnesstohistory.com/fdrdeath.htm
[74] http://time.com/3764064/mourning-fdr-in-a-classic-photo-the-face-of-a-nations-loss/

Would the war end? How? When? V-E day came on May 7 [75] and all the Allies had to do now was defeat Japan, a formidable task.

For some unknown reason, it was time to move on. School was out and we needed to move to the pea fields of Eastern Oregon to work the crops and earn money. We moved in style this time. Dad bought a used 22-foot travel trailer, a real luxury after sleeping in the car or on the ground during all the other moves. It was blue and grey, primitive by the standards of our present Country Coach, but Mom believed it was Cinderella's castle.

The sides were Masonite [76] and there were windows that opened and closed. There was a propane stove and a small refrigerator plus a table for dining. It could sleep five. Mom and Dad had the bed in back. The kitchen table was converted to a bed at night, hard as concrete, for Tom and me. Poor Caroline got the floor between the two sleeping zones. No toilet but we had a handy White Owl for nighttime contributions. It was usually full as a deacon's plate and foaming in the morning. It was frequently my job to empty it. No worry about black and grey holding tanks in those days. Just go ahead and pollute the aquifer.

The small Talent house was sold. The new occupants came and began installing indoor plumbing before we had even packed the house trailer. We departed north up Highway 99 and then east beyond Portland over the old Columbia Gorge Highway 30 [77] to Milton-Freewater, a farming area in the Northeast corner of Oregon.[78] Once again, we were going somewhere.

Mom said we could have another summer adventure in the pea fields, but would need to be settled before September so "Jimmy" could start school and my siblings could finish their public education in one city. Poor Caroline and Tom never had that concern, but that may be why they are more adaptable than I and make friends easier. Regardless how and where we lived, we turned out okay. My family never regretted any of these migratory years during World War II. The world was changing and we were a part of it. The war was soon to end and we were all going to be flying around in personal flying machines strapped to our backs,[79] which was predicted by some visionaries.

---

[75] http://www.historylearningsite.co.uk/world-war-two/world-war-two-in-western-europe/ve-day/
[76] https://en.wikipedia.org/wiki/Masonite
[77] http://traveloregon.com/trip-ideas/scenic-byways/the-historic-columbia-river-highway/
[78] https://en.wikipedia.org/wiki/Milton-Freewater,_Oregon
[79] http://www.telegraph.co.uk/film/tomorrowland/walt-disneys-predictions/

Chapter 6   Pea-ing in Milton-Freewater

Much like all the other moves, there seemed to be little motivation for the next one, other than to find work. Travel was wonderful with a house trailer. We could stop for real meals at noon and sit at a table. Food could be cooked and served. Milk from Tiny and Betty could be chilled. We all loved the trailer house, especially Mom. Things were in place from day to day.

The trip from Talent to Milton-Freewater took several days. Picture my father driving the Ford truck towing a house trailer and my mother driving a Studebaker towing a trailer with two cows and a host of chickens. The I-84 freeway was 20 years in the future, so the road took us from Portland, out Sandy Boulevard through Parkrose, and then up to Crown Point,[80] where we were told there was a million dollar toilet. We never got to use it, though, because we then drove down the loops and on the scenic road to Cascade Locks and the newly opened Bonneville Dam.[81] Then the road took us through a series of tunnels around Mitchell Point, Hood River and Mosier. This was old Highway 30, now a scenic byway.

We traversed the crooked and dangerous Rowena switchbacks, after which the road leveled somewhat as the Columbia gorge widened. Eventually, we arrived at Milton-Freewater. Dad immediately procured a job driving truck for a pea factory. Tom was now 15 and could obtain a permit to work in the pea fields. Mom worked in the cannery. We camped on a hill above the pea cannery, near the tiny town of Milton-Freewater. Apparently it was a public area and we were never harassed by authorities to move on.

Caroline, now 12 years old, babysat me on those days when everyone was working. Those days were long and we managed to got into mischief, hiding in the bushes near the cannery and making farting noises as the women walked home after their shift. Although we were pretty vulgar, much to our disappointment we were generally ignored by those we were trying to startle. At times, Dad would drive by in his truck and throw a host of pea vines to us. This was a signal to quickly gather the vines together, pick the pods and shell them. The cows ate the vines. Fresh peas were part of the evening meal and Mom probably canned a few jars in preparation for winter.

---

[80] http://www.oregonstateparks.org/index.cfm?do=parkPage.dsp_parkPage&parkId=108

[81] http://columbiariverimages.com/Regions/Places/bonneville_dam.html

Where would we spend the winter of 1945? It was already August and the war in the Pacific was still waging. It seemed an invasion of Japan would be necessary; costing innumerable military and civilian lives as well as massive devastation of the Japanese islands. However, the newspapers reported the advent of the Atomic Age [82] when the bomb was dropped on Hiroshima on August 6, Nagasaki on August 9. By then we were on our way to Portland for Dad to search for work on the docks. But we never made it.

Twenty miles west of Hood River, a tire on the Ford V-8 gave out and we pulled into Lindsey Creek, [83] a picnic area on the Columbia River, to lick our wounds and strategize how to obtain a new tire. Gas was low and both rubber and fuel were rationed. Lindsey Creek was a lovely area, peaceful and quiet, with clean flowing water. (Even Lewis and Clark had commented on this area in their diaries.) The chickens could feed free-range and there was grass for the cows, which meant milk for us. We were safe in the trailer but knew we had to move on to obtain a job and housing before school began after Labor Day. Dad and Tom hitchhiked to Portland, leaving the car, which needed gas, for Mom. Dad was certain there would be work for a stevedore on the Portland docks.

At Lindsey Creek, Caroline and I crossed the road and bathed in the Columbia River just beyond, which was near the Union Pacific rail line. Troop trains going east and west frequently came through, traveling quite slowly. They were often sidelined to allow another train to pass. We would banter with the troops and enjoyed their rude, provocative shouts, since guys can be bold when they are in big groups and have the safety of no face-to-face encounters. However, on August 15, [84] just as we were walking towards the moving train. They shouted: "The war is over." Japan unconditionally surrendered after the two atomic bomb assaults. Two cities were devastated, thousands of lives lost immediately and many more as radiation set in. This was the brave new world but it was not as brave as we had all anticipated. However, now families could obtain some degree of normality and that certainly happened for ours. Our nomadic existence ended at Lindsey Creek in mid-August, 1945.

While hitching a ride back from Portland, Dad and Tom were picked up by a congenial contractor, Jack B., from Hood River in a 1940s-something Buick. Help was scarce and he knew a man, Larry B., who owned the country club outside of Hood River. Could Dad manage a golf resort? If so, we might be welcome to move our trailer, truck, car and

---

[82] http://alsos.wlu.edu/history.aspx
[83] http://columbiariverimages.com/Regions/Places/lindsey_creek.html
[84] http://www.history.com/topics/world-war-ii/v-j-day

cows next to an abandoned house near the greens. Rent would be free and there would be wages.

Tire was repaired and gas obtained, so we somehow got to Hood River and met with Larry B., who allegedly had won the golf course in a poker game. There was a job for Dad as course manager. Even Tom might earn a few dollars as his assistant and Mom could be used in kitchen for social events. It was not a house but Hood River would become our home for the next six years as we began to put down roots in one place. It was closer to Yakima than anything yet experienced on this incredible journey but a long, long way from Los Angeles.

We were only at the golf resort for three weeks, but it was nice to be in a safe environment with friendly golfers, who tipped generously when Caroline and I retrieved their golf balls lost in the rough. The weather was warm and soft, as it can be along the Columbia Gorge in summer. We spent time out-of-doors. Dad was highly successful as a manager of the greens but needed a job that brought in more money. My mother wanted a real home, not a house trailer. And school was beginning.

Chapter 7   Never Hesitate: Just Fumigate!

At the end of August, it was time to find a house. Housing was scarce during the war and immediately after. It took a while after the troops came home from both war theaters to get construction moving again and ramping up the economy. But it was a time of reunion for families, with marriages and a boom in baby production. Even the popular music of the time reflected the long separation endured by couples throughout the war, their dreams while apart and finally their joyful reunions. [85]

Home building during the Great Depression was 10% of what it had been during the booming 1920's, so there was pent-up demand for affordable housing. Consumer goods like cars and washing machines came back on the market, triggered by nine million servicemen [86] coming home, marrying and seeking shelter.

We learned there was a vacant house on Markham Lane, about five miles south of Hood River in an area called Rockford. It could be rented for $11 a month. It was small and old. Most critically, the last tenant had died of diphtheria, which was contagious, so it needed to be fumigated. Although fumigation was common in California, where the house would be tented with a large canvas to destroy infestations of termites, it was rarely used in Oregon. Fumigation could possibly destroy all vestiges of diphtheria and bed bugs of the former inhabitant as well as morally cleanse the premises.   And Dad did it. He entered the house and lit several little candles [87] with wicks that released fumes and smoke throughout the building, destroying all those germs as well as anything else that was going to bite or blight us. The house was so rickety and full of holes that most of the smoke escaped through every knothole and ceiling joist, since he did not use tenting. It looked like we had set the house on fire, our own little Dresden [88] casualty at Rockford.   A day later, the smoke began to clear. We pulled our trailer in front, released the cows into the five-acre pasture and set up residency.

An absentee landlady to whom Dad sent the $11 rent check monthly for several years owned the property. It was not much of a house. There was a living area with an old pot-bellied wood heater plus a small kitchen that would accommodate our Wedgewood [89] wood range, which we had

---

[85] https://library.syr.edu/belfer/programs/projects/belfer78/

[86] https://en.wikipedia.org/wiki/Demobilization_of_United_States_armed_forces_after_World_War_II

[87] http://www.dave-cushman.net/bee/fumcandle.html

[88] http://www.history.com/this-day-in-history/firebombing-of-dresden

[89] http://www.antiquegasstoves.com/pages/wedgewood.html

faithfully carried in the Ford truck all these years. It required a new water heater tank to connect to the coils of the stove, if we wanted hot water. There was running water, thanks to a hand pump, but the one kitchen sink drained through an old pipe into the back yard. The EPA [90] was not around to monitor such conditions and, after all, it was merely gray water.

There was no indoor plumbing but a massive privy sat two hundred feet from the house with a three-hole station and an energetic resident rat. It was air-conditioned naturally, much like the house. There was plenty of room for a Sears and Roebuck catalog, should one need reading material on a morning trip. In the house, there was a small alcove off the kitchen that would accommodate a larger bed. In addition to Mom and Dad's bed, Tom's bed from California was in the truck, and both were assembled in the shack. Caroline and I would sleep on folding army cots, opened each night and closed during the day, unless they were called on to serve as a sofa.

Bathing would be accomplished in a round washtub.[91] There were no taking turns on the bath water. One hot bath was drawn on Saturday night for the kids and there was a strict hierarchy how it was allotted. As the youngest child, I was always the third user. By then, the water was pretty cold as well as rather soapy. But we stayed clean. But it is a wonder I did not foam in the rain, however, from soap film buildup.

The house was not finished inside, but had rough-surfaced two-by-fours as ceiling joists and studs. The floor was a single layer of rough planks, 1" by 12"s elevated somewhat from the ground with rocks and old bricks. It sagged in places and had numerous holes, some covered with a nailed-down rusty top of a can, others, wide open. In short, it was nothing more than a shack. It could not have been more than 500 square feet, which was about half the size of a typical home in 1945.[92] There was no insulation, no R-factor, no structural support. It rocked in the wind.

Although wired for electricity, it was a nightmare waiting to happen with exposed lines and poor fittings. Light came from glaring incandescent bulbs screwed into ceiling-mounted porcelain fixtures. These were illuminated by a pull-string or merely by screwing in the bulb. We received light as well as from the inadvertent skylights in the roof, that is, knotholes, at least until Dad fixed those. There was no breaker box,

---

[90] http://www3.epa.gov
[91] http://www.sears.com/round-tub/p-00894414000P?sid=IDx01192011x000001&pla&kpid=00894414000&kispla=00894414000P
[92] http://www2.census.gov/prod2/popscan/p60-002.pdf

just a series of glass fuses that melted if too much demand were placed on a line, which happened daily. Dad learned to put in a higher-amperage fuse to mitigate. Some of our interior heating undoubtedly came from overloaded and exposed wires.

Nonetheless, it a was roof over our head and we had the trailer house for a while in which to live, at least until we sold it to a couple bound for the University of Oregon on the GI Bill. Mom was determined we would begin school the day after Labor Day, September 4, 1945.

As Eleanor Roosevelt declared on this Labor Day:

> *We are entering an era, I think, when there will be increasingly less room in the world for those who do not wish to work. There is so much to be done now, and any civilization or form of government which does not find a way to put the work that needs to be done within the reach of those who want to do it is no longer going to be tolerated.*
>
> *That, it seems to me, is why Labor Day this year has a special significance. Labor has grown up. It is a powerful section of the community, and it must share the responsibility of shaping the future. It must sit down at the same table with the heads of industries and plan for the acceptance of legislation, which will make full employment possible and for the way since which such legislation shall be implemented by the joint effort of labor and capital.*
>
> *The ends that must be achieved to give the people of our nation work and health and happiness grow out of the acceptance of the right to work, and the obligation of all governments to so organize a civilized economy that this right shall not be denied to anyone anywhere.*[93]

Tom, in new Levis, smart and shiny loafers and a spiffy looking striped t-shirt, Caroline in a store-bought dress and me in new cotton bibbed-overalls with a clean shirt posed in front of our trailer for a picture on September 4, 1945, before heading off to school. I was a first-grader and Caroline was in the seventh grade at Barrett Elementary,[94] one-half mile from our house. Tom was off to the bus-head to begin his sophomore

---

[93]

[94] http://m.hoodrivernews.com/news/2003/aug/13/remembering-mrs-yeck-and-a-beloved-old-school/

year at Hood River High School, [95] home of the mighty Dragons. We looked tentatively grateful that the nomadic life was over and we were now permanent citizens of a post-war community. Dad landed a good job at the Jaymar Lumber Mill [96] in Hood River on the Columbia River.[97] Everyone was off to something new.

There were no nearby rail tracks in Rockford. Maybe that is why we lived there five and a half years. You could not hear nearby trains. But we did have a panoramic view of Mt. Adams in Washington state, much like it appears in the Percy Manser murals [98] at Hood River High School's auditorium. That majestic view continues to be etched in my memory and I have always had a special attraction to the volcanoes in the Cascade Range of the Pacific Northwest.

---

[95] https://commons.wikimedia.org/wiki/File:Hood_River_Middle_School_north_face_-_Hood_River_Oregon.jpg
[96] http://historichoodriver.com/index.php?showimage=1224
[97] http://historichoodriver.com/index.php?showimage=580
[98] http://www.art-first.com/11_Historic_paint_colors_Historic_building_restoration_Historic_murals.html

Chapter 8   Unknown Garrett at Barrett

There really was a garret at Barrett Elementary. It was the top middle room of the second-story, where kids would be chosen to ring the mighty school bell by pulling on a rope. I think I was able to do that several times in my five and a half years as a student there. It was a reward to be chosen to pull that rope, much like stars or flower stickers on a lesson well achieved. You had to produce to be rewarded. Just being part of a group did not mean you deserved a blue ribbon. Unlike Lake Woebegone,[99] only some children were above average, others were average. We learned being average does not diminish one's value as a human being. But one could be held back if he or she failed a grade. Social promotion was not yet a popular scheme.

No pre-school in those days. No Kindergarten. No play dates. First grade was my first exposure to many kids my age. For someone who would end up spending eight years in elementary school, four in high school. four in undergraduate studies, nine years earning three advanced degrees and then 42 years in a classroom as a teacher, I did not want to go to school. It makes one believe a person who faints at the sight of blood could still become an effective surgeon.

I never have received my energy from being around other people and this might have been an early manifestation of that trait. I cried when Mom left me. Caroline, who was in the seventh grade classroom above me, checked on me at recess and the noon hour while I ate a peanut butter and jelly sandwich on Bimbo bread. By the end of the day, after we were able to do some artwork, I thought I could endure school for another day.

Then I was hooked. It was a magical room with letters and numbers, bright colored construction paper, safe scissors, chalk and blackboards, books, charts, LePage paste [100] (that could be tasted) and a gentle teacher, Miss F. All I had to supply was a box of crayons. My box was minimal, maybe eight to ten sticks, but I observed some children had bigger boxes with a multitude of colors. Others had none at all. They must have not read the memo.

I don't remember much about this teacher because she was only there for a short time until Miss D., a former Army nurse, took over the class. She had been delayed mustering out from the Army so a substitute had taken her place for the early school year. Miss D. was classy, tall and slim, and she drove a new 1945 Ford two-door sedan. There was a variety of students, probably 30 or more in my class, some of them

---

[99] http://www.brainyquote.com/quotes/quotes/g/garrisonke137097.html
[100] http://www.jeffs60s.com/school.php

dressed well and some not so well, smelling of things I had never experienced, whether expensive soap and new clothes, onions, bed clothing or simply urine.

We were all aware of Mrs. Y., [101] the school principal, who taught the combined seventh and eighth grade classroom upstairs. She was to be respected and feared. School administrators in those days were simply senor teachers, not certified professionals. You could be sent to Mrs. Y. if you did something wrong, which might result in standing in the corner, wearing a dunce hat or even being paddled with a yard stick as you laid prostrate over a wooden desk.

I loved the little desks. They were all attached in rows [102] and each room had a different size, depending on the grade. I would sit in Caroline's desk upstairs and could hardly reach the floor with my feet, my chin resting on the desktop. But mine was perfect for a first grader. There was a hole for ink, but that did not come until fourth grade. The tops opened to reveal your contents of books, papers, artwork and lunch. The seats folded upwards. There were no cubbies, only a cloakroom with a swinging door to hang your coat and store galoshes on rainy days until school was dismissed. The doors to the classrooms were also swinging. No need to secure the classroom from intruders armed with AK-47s.[103]

I knew my alphabet but could not read at age six and a half. But no one could. Miss D. used little books with lots of pictures and a few words to introduce reading. I would look at the book, see the same symbols on charts above the blackboard, and realize it meant something. The stories, which she read to us, were about things children would know, dogs, cats, children, cars.

Dick and Jane and a dog named Spot were always part of the scene.[104] They were well dressed, middle-class Anglos, which reflected the culture around us, at least in terms of skin color and socio-economic class. That was the way Scott Foresman [105] saw the American family in 1945: Mom, Dad, two delightful, well-dressed children, always one boy and one girl, and a well-behaved dog living in a lovely home in the post-war world. Most of us had a long way to go to achieve it, whether as a family or a nation.

---

[101] http://m.hoodrivernews.com/news/2003/aug/13/remembering-mrs-yeck-and-a-beloved-old-school/
[102] http://billchance.org/2012/08/07/old-school/
[103] https://en.wikipedia.org/wiki/AK-47
[104] https://en.wikipedia.org/wiki/Dick_and_Jane
[105] https://en.wikipedia.org/wiki/Scott_Foresman

Around the middle of October, it all clicked and I was reading. I don't know when it happened nor do I remember the process. It just happened. Those words represented what I was seeing in the pictures. Language was basically the names of things and the actions of what the things did. There were even commands: "Look"; "See"; "Come". The colors in the classroom were predominantly orange and black, so it must have been close to Halloween. It was as wonderful to me as deciphering the Rosetta Stone [106] or as Helen Keller making the connection between the water she was ingesting with Annie Sullivan's hand gesture.[107] In our analytic age, processes do not need to be parsed to be valid. Intuition is still critical in learning and becoming more human.

There was lots of poverty in my grades, old clothes, lack of hygiene, bad teeth, and ragged clothes. There was a hot lunch program, which cost $2.00 a month, but poor children were never denied food. My mother would have gone vertical if I had forgotten to pay my monthly $2.00, which she faithfully allotted the first school day of each month. We never really noticed poverty, except when it was contrasted with wealth.

There was one princess who was the daughter of a wealthy fruit rancher. She had a close circle of friends, all girls, who surrounded her and granted her every wish and want. She led their play and was a class leader, not necessarily by brains but by beauty and possessions. Her teeth were perfect from good genetics and excellent nutrition. Although she was nice, she was distant to most of us. I met her again years later when we were both out of high school. She turned out to be a real beauty with a personality to match. The princess thing had somewhat dissipated. She could have attended any college she wanted, but she married out of high school and became a mother. She probably inherited well from all the orchards her parents owned.

Barrett was a big brick building, red in color, built in 1910. There was nothing significant about its structure, since it was a carbon copy of many schools of that period. Oak Grove School in the valley and Park Street School in downtown Hood River were similar.[108] The main building had two classrooms on each floor.

On the first floor, there was a large gymnasium at the back end with a stage. Down the stairs were bathrooms for each gender, which also led to a long hallway. This housed two additional classrooms, which were added later. These rooms had moveable desks. The fourth and fifth graders and some sixth graders were down there, while the main floor

---

[106] https://en.wikipedia.org/wiki/Rosetta_Stone
[107] http://www.biography.com/people/anne-sullivan-9498826
[108] http://historichoodriver.com/index.php?showimage=714

had first-second graders on one side, second-third graders on the other. The rest of the sixth grade and all the seventh-eighth graders were in the upper two classrooms. There were six teachers, all women, in 1945. Male teachers had not yet been mustered out from the troops. Teachers split grades to share the burden but in retrospect, they were probably streaming kids according to abilities.

The playground was extensive, three or four acres, with a large, covered play shed for those rainy Hood River Valley days. There were woodpiles to fuel the enormous furnace buried somewhere in the bowels of this massive building. There were outside fire escapes running from each of the classrooms in the main building, just like a scene from *West Side Story*.[109] It was a precarious path to safety for the older students, should disaster strike. We used these ladders during frequent fire drills but never during a real fire.

Once the school did catch on fire but it was early in the morning, when the janitor was stoking a massive fire to heat the building. We could see the roof of the school from our shack on Markham Lane. The sawmill was closed and Dad was drinking coffee at home on a snowy winter morning. He looked out the window and saw smoke rising from old Barrett. He got in the Studebaker and zoomed to the school, went up onto the roof and doused the fire. Sparks had ignited some of the roof shingles. The school board and teachers were appreciative, but Caroline and I became less popular on the playground for the next several weeks. It did not burn and school was held that day. Eventually it did burn, long after it had ceased to be a public school, somewhat reminiscent of the fire in the symbolic church in John Updike's novel, *Couples*.[110]

Barrett was a happy school experience for my first five years in school as well as half of my sixth grade. My sister, in the seventh grade while I was in the first, was in attendance for the first two years. If I got in trouble and was kept after school, she would peer into the classroom at me, head down on my desk, and I knew I would be in double trouble when I got home. I never was because she rarely tattled. And she was always in enough trouble herself that she probably thought I would tattle on her when we got home. As a first or second grader, I was out earlier and would wait for her to walk home with me. She was a little mother and an incredible protector. She knew some pretty good swear words that no one in our family was allowed to use, except Dad, and only then when he was angry.

---

[109] https://en.wikipedia.org/wiki/West_Side_Story
[110] https://en.wikipedia.org/wiki/Couples_(novel)

She graduated the eighth grade in 1947. Her class consisted of six girls, many with whom she has remained friends, and each girl had a brand new store-bought dress to wear at the ceremony. Students only graduated grade school, not every grade, and mortarboards were unheard of until high school graduation.

In the third grade and through the sixth, I was on my own at Barrett Elementary. The teachers were wonderful. Mrs. Nellie R. was my second and third grade teacher. We were members of the Valley Christian Church, as was Mrs. R. and her family. She drove a new Oldsmobile each year because her spouse had the local dealership in Hood River. She had a lively, if slightly wicked sense of humor.

One child in the second grade made all-too frequent lavatory visits, which might have been from diarrhea, a small bladder or just boredom with the classroom. Mrs. R. decided to toy with him a little when he returned to the classroom, advising we were going to play a joke. There was a huge swinging oak door for entering the classroom. When we thought this kid was returning, the door was pushed in a bit. Mrs. R. pushed back, denying entrance. This pushing and pulling went on for a few seconds until she decided to let him in. The door swung open and in walked Mrs. Y., the principal. Mrs. R. became very serious and we kids at our desks immediately returned to Dick and Jane.

Mrs. R. loved art but we only got to do it on Friday afternoons, which was very common in elementary schools. You could move about the room and interact with other children. Parents sent candy for these Friday sessions, at least many did, including the fruit farm princess, whose largesse always outshone the offerings of us from less affluent households. But my parents always sent something and all gratefully received it.

Mrs. R.'s daughter, Helen, a well-educated college graduate was to be married at Valley Christian Church. Mom was the church pianist and was asked to play for the wedding. No fee was proffered because she was the church pianist, if only on a volunteer basis. Mrs. R. and Helen came to our house to plan the music. They were invited to sit on the orange crates we used for chairs. (They also were great storage devices if one covered the front with a curtain, which we did.) The plan for the wedding music was drawn up, much as if the festivities had been arranged at the local country club.

The wedding was held, the cake was cut and we threw rice as the happy couple exited for a honeymoon on the Oregon coast. The next week, a pick-up truck driven by Mrs. R.'s son, Earl, and her husband, Simon, delivered a used but expensive sofa to our house. My mother cried but we three kids put our butts on something comfortable for a change. Mrs. R. was generous to a fault to her friends, family and students.

At age ten, on March 9, 1949, I was baptized by emersion (dunking, Dad always said) and became a Christian. Rev. Lawrence P. did the dunking and the water was cold. In school the next day, Mrs. R. relayed this story to my reading group. She was a saint who didn't have fear about proclaiming her Christian love to everyone, whether in the classroom or not. You didn't have to worry about being religious in those days, whether Protestant or Catholic. We didn't know anyone who was Jewish, anyway, and Muslims were something of which we had never heard.

School was easy for me. I was in the top reading group and mastered most concepts easily. If I got in trouble, it was usually because I had finished the minimal assignments and was bothering others. My mouth has always gotten me in trouble. Most teachers encouraged additional projects in other texts or let me do art projects. There was a question whether I should skip a grade, but few kids actually did that and I didn't want to leave my classmates. At times, I was given the responsibility to hear other kids read in a lower-level reading group, particularly when there were mixed grades in one classroom. I loved that experience. It was a natural fit for me and teachers were willing to give me that responsibility. Good thing I did love it. I ended up doing it most of my life, one way or another.

A male teacher came to Barrett in my fourth or fifth grade so we began to have organized physical education. Mr. B. became the new principal when Mrs. Y. retired. He drove a diminutive Crosley [111] car, a new breed of post-war auto production. His spouse was from New Hampshire, with an accent so thick that we all thought she was speaking a foreign language when she substituted.

Boys were beginning to chase girls and girls were beginning to tantalize boys. Hormones allowed it. Sex was never discussed in my family, but I knew what it was, even if I was not certain how often or why it occurred. Childhood innocence ended around the fifth grade in those days. One had to be with a pack of guys, if male, or girls, if female. Anything else provoked snickers and teasing.

We had to play basketball with the older students, skins versus shirts, and I was always a skin. My sensitive skin, which I inherited from my father, had red spots. It looked like I had measles and it alarmed my classmates. It was a great source of teasing. I was probably anemic, but we did not go to the doctor to check it out. Doctors cost money and

---

[111] https://en.wikipedia.org/wiki/Crosley

my affliction was only cosmetic, not physical. I think my mother, who only reluctantly ever sent notes to school, requested I be a shirt in P.E., not a skin. I didn't play basketball any better but gym time was less stressful.

Lucky for me, P.E. was only once or twice a week, or whenever Mr. B. was freed from classroom duties. This was my first experience with a male teacher, my first experience with an adult male other than my father. Basically, a mother, an older sister, school and church teachers, who were all females, had raised me. To make matters worse, in my neighborhood, my only close friends within a half-mile were all girls. I could not play very often with neighbor Lowell H., a year younger than I. Mom felt the family was not clean. My mother always said not to eat anything when I was at their house. But once, while playing there, Opal H. offered a piece of chocolate to each of us kids. I ate it and knew I was going to die within a few hours, if not from germs, then from my mother's interrogation when I returned home. Later, Lowell contracted polio and that affirmed mother's insistence. But then it could have been polio lurking in an irrigation ditch, a common belief at that time.

My only other male role model was my brother, nine years my senior. In my formative years, he was busy becoming an adult. In those years, I did not develop the sports mentality and physical dexterity many boys develop. There was no football, no baseball, just basketball from time to time. Many families had relatives who practiced sports like touch football in their backyards. Mine did not. I never really believed I had any athletic ability until I was middle aged. And thank goodness schools now have volleyball, pickleball, golf, soccer, swimming and track and field events for both boys and girls.

Chapter 9   Enhance Household Finance

If there were a chance to earn money, my Mom and Dad were on it. In the Barrett years, Dad had steady work at the Jaymar Lumber Mill. Many of the men in our neighborhood also worked there. Only in the winter, when the woods shut down and the ponds froze was the mill closed. He received some unemployment benefits during that time. When the mill was running, he took all the overtime he could, often working ten to twelve hours a day, while still tending milk cows and pigs on our five acres in Rockford. Tom and Caroline, however, were pretty good about helping in the barnyard. Everyone had chores to accomplish the daily routines.

As I became older, I fed the chickens and gathered the eggs after I walked home from school. There was no homework. It was all accomplished in the classroom, so there was no backpack of books to carry back and forth each day. Caroline was the champion milkmaid, making the liquid sing against the side of the pail. She and Dad would each sit at the side of one of our cows and play a sprightly two-part invention until their pails were full.

I tried to learn to milk, but the cows became very impatient with me, swishing their tails the minute I sat down. They would then move their hind legs as if they were going to kick me if I didn't leave. However, they were gentle creatures, much beloved in our family. We had stud service for them each year to produce a calf, hopefully a bull, which would become our winter meat. Dad would slaughter the beast, deliver it to a butcher in town who would cut it up, wrap and label it. Packages of meat would be placed in a frozen locker in Hood River, since personal freezers were not yet available. Most of this beef had been pets before, so the meat was not easy to swallow.

The pent-up demand for consumer goods after the war and rising wages allowed us to purchase a new refrigerator during these years. It was a white Norge,[112] not big by today's standards, but much nicer than the old fridge that had followed us from California. I loved that Norge. It looked big to me, but probably was only ten cubic feet. It had a little freezer inside which held ice cube trays but could store a quart of ice cream at pudding consistency. There was a clock on its door, so the Big Ben was not the only source of diurnal movement in our house. And white was the appliance designer color of the late 1940's. Actually, it was the only color.

---

[112] http://laundry.reviewed.com/features/5-extinct-appliance-brands-that-died-too-soon

Neighbors were buying new cars, shiny, colorful machines with turtle backs, automatic transmissions and lots of chrome. The G.s, who lived across the street in a nice house, owned the Pontiac dealership in Hood River. They were kind to us and I played with their youngest child, Judith, one year older than I. The neighborhood protocol, which my mother instituted, was to say how long you could "play", or better yet, "stay", when you went to a friend's house. You would announce this out of the chute and the host would remind you when to leave. For me, it was half an hour, but, at times, a full hour. That way, the welcome was never worn out. If my visitors did not follow this procedure, my mother, nonetheless, would remind them to leave. No hanging around in those days because there were chores to do.

The G.s took a rode trip to Yellowstone National Park one summer, which seemed as far away as Europe to me. When they returned with a multitude of 35 mm slides, all the neighbors were invited to their home to see a travel presentation. It was followed by homemade ice cream, which was more like pudding than ice cream. They had an electric churner while my family had an old crank type. Both turned out good desserts but ours always took longer. The rich cream from our cows made far superior ice cream.

Judith had three older brothers but they never played with me. They were a team and participated in activities as a family unit, not needing a snotty-nosed neighbor kid who lived in a shack as part of their close-knit activities. Judith's mother Vivian was patrician, slight and dainty, and she would correct my behavior in her house or yard, kindly but firmly at all times.

One Halloween, right before we moved from Rockford, I was in a dilemma about trick or treating. Judith and I had always gone together, dressed in homemade costumes with a mask that practically smothered you. She was now in the seventh grade, had boy friends and was not into childlike things. I planned to go on this annual excursion myself, but the day before, she came to my house and said we would be going together. "We always have", she said. "No costumes this year, just regular clothes because we're older." I was both delighted and devastated; delighted I would have company but devastated I would not be able to wear my costume.

In the 1940s, Halloween was a kid's holiday, not for adults. One would not see adults in restaurants, banks and grocery stores dressed as the Mad Hatter or Dracula. It was not a time to act out your fantasy. You simply knocked on doors, received a homemade treat, graciously thanked the neighbors who would comment on your costume and then moved on to the next house. We ate the largesse all without running it through a metal detector. And there never were "tricks" to the houses, which had their porch lights extinguished.

There were always parties at Halloween at school but one year I was informed, mistakenly, that we could not have costumes. I had taken mine that day but hid it for fear of getting in trouble. As it turned out, the older students all came down the hall in costumes and it was too late for me to don mine. I learned then to double-check the memo before I made a strategic decision. Lesson learned.

Around the time I was nine or ten, Mom decided to get a job, at least a seasonal job. The abundance of the fruit crops in the Hood River Valley required a work force to pick the fruit, but, more importantly, to prepare it for shipment outside the state and even overseas. It was reported over 24,000 workers were needed for the state's fruit industry, 1000 women and 400 men [113] in the Hood River area alone, according to the A.G.A., or Apple Growers Association. That meant the pears and apples were brought to a packing shed in lug boxes on a truck bed. Sorters sat by conveyor belts and plucked out fruit of poor quality and minimal size. The fruit then dropped into round bins by size where packers would place a wooden box on a holding stand, grab individual pieces, wrap each in paper and place in a box with precision. [114]

My mother was young, only 38, and she thought she would be a sorter. Sorters were paid by the hour. The wages were probably less than $1.00 per hour and older women did this. She was encouraged to learn to pack. There was even a school to teach the skill. It was piecework and more money could be earned, payment for each box produced. It was hard work but Mom was a good packer. She did it for over 20 years.

Fruit was sized by the number of pieces that would fit into a wooden box.[115] Size 120 meant 120 pears or apples in a box, carefully wrapped in treated paper, which would reduce spoilage, and then placed in a geometric design, slightly crowned at the top. It was beautiful work but stressful. Big pears were heavy and smaller ones, like 180s, required more work to fill a box. Packers rotated around the bins every half hour so that no one always had the same sized fruit. [116]

---

[113] http://www.hoodrivernews.com/news/2015/aug/12/yesteryears-packing-houses-need-workers-1945/
[114] http://oregonhistoryproject.org/articles/historical-records/crating-apples-in-hood-river/#.Vq_aS4T0iDk
[115] https://en.wikipedia.org/wiki/Packing_house
[116] http://oregonhistoryproject.org/articles/historical-records/crating-apples-in-hood-river/#.Vqwe8oT0iDk

The fast packers, who could turn out 150-200 boxes a day, appreciated my mother. If she could not empty the bins when the fruit was pouring in, she would call for a "swing" packer. This person would come beside her and help empty the bin, two persons wrapping and filling two boxes. Each box received the individual packer's stamp, which was then tallied on a rolling track before being lidded and shipped out. If the box were not crowned or had a weight discrepancy, the packer had to retrieve it at day's end and make it right. Mom had the reputation as an almost "perfect" packer because she did not rush as she worked. Rarely were her boxes sidetracked for remedial attention at the end of the day.

Mom was not fast, but she could churn out a hundred packed boxes on a good day. This was how fruit was prepared for distribution to other markets in the late 1940s. It was the beginning of an international food distribution system that would eventually bring us fruits and vegetables from all over the world anytime of the year. Mom was part of that incipient system. Throughout her career as a packer, the Asian markets opened, requiring fruit to be almost flawless. In addition, the construction of cold storage sheds throughout the industry allowed growers and distributors to control the market beyond harvest time. It also made packing a year-long job, since fruit for shipping could be taken out of storage and packed in late spring as easily as during the fall harvest. Mom's seasonal job for a few months in September and October eventually turned into one that provided work six to nine months of year.

Japanese-American farmers were returning to the Hood River Valley and reclaiming their orchards after years of internment. One very bright Japanese girl lived up the street from us and her family had a large orchard. Mitzi A. was (and still is) a friend with my sister. However, the prejudice and hatred generated during the war did not dissipate easily among all our neighbors. I remember this young girl walking home from Barrett School and being assaulted with rocks and profanity as she passed one house every night. She learned to run. The local store proprietor would not allow her in his store to purchase candy after school. Interestingly enough, she grew up to be a professor of French in her life pursuit.

The thrust of Mom's employment was that we had more money. She had pocket money, seemingly lots of it. We all got allowances, based on our age, and it came every Friday after she received her weekly check. I still had chores to accomplish but the two were not connected. My daily chores were to build the fire when I got home, gather the eggs, and set the table. I would also start the dinner, if something could be warmed over. My allowance was ten cents a week and it was given without restriction on how it was used. I could buy candy, I could save for a toy or book or I could save it in the bank.

Saving was encouraged and I had a small account at the First National Bank with a bankbook with hand-written entries. It was a source of pride for me as well. We also learned at this time we kids each had a war-bond, that when it expired, would be worth $25. Dad had purchased these in California when the war began. It was hardly a 529-college fund but it certainly demonstrated the need to save for the future and the power of compound interest, minimal as it was (and still is) in those days. Why would someone pay you money for a deposit? I learned why long before I earned my M.B.A.

Tom was driving by now and was not as involved with family functions as earlier. He had a host of friends including a variety of girl friends. The Studebaker sedan was never at home on Saturday nights but I remember more than once Dad firing up the Ford V-8 to pull the sedan out of a ditch. Seems Tom was the one-person driver-education instructor for the high school, teaching all of his friends to drive on the old Studebaker. Dad would grumble about these weekend excursions but always fetched the old car, spouting edgy oaths coming and going. I do not know how Tom cried for help, but it probably meant walking home several miles and waking Dad. Walking was something we all did, except when we used the bicycle.

It was this ill-assembled bike that delivered a dessert to the local bake sale with more fiber than originally intended. Barrett School's annual bazaar needed a pie and we had blackberries. Mom did her usual delight, probably baking two, one for the family and one for the school function. If you were going to heat the wood stove's oven, might as well make it worth your while. Her crusts were impeccable and she would place strips of the dough across the top of the pie in crisscross fashion. It looked glorious. Tom and Caroline would now deliver it, he pedaling on the bike seat, she holding the pie tightly with one hand as she balanced the other on the handlebars.

Markham Lane had potholes and a direct hit with the front wheel of the old bike sent the pie sky high, returning to earth on the gravel shoulder. It was scooped up, gravel and all, sort of rearranged to look edible and delivered to the school cafeteria sans explanation. Mom was not aware of these shenanigans for years, but she did ponder why organizers requested she send only cookies for future bake sales.

I loved the movies and it only cost fourteen cents to attend a double feature at the Rialto [117] or Cascadian in Hood River. The movies changed three times a week, which meant six offerings (movies were only about

---

[117] http://historichoodriver.com/index.php?showimage=1069

60-90 minutes) and I usually got to see one or two each week. In order for Tom to get access to the Studebaker, he said he would take me to the movies. Actually, he would drop me off, pick up his latest girl friend and then retrieve me after the second movie. He knew the attendants and they would come into the theater to get me. There was usually a girl friend in tow and I would have to wait in the car while he walked her to the front door and kissed her good night. I never told, because the movie excursions were my great escape from being at home all the time.

My brother, so he claimed, was the "stud of Hood River". There were no pregnancies nor shot gun weddings, so it may have been more locker-room bravado than reality. Nonetheless, when we shared a bedroom later, he had an ample supply of Sheiks and Trojans in his personal space. In those days, condoms were cheap and came without elaborate packaging, glitzy foil in designer colors, as they are now. I do know he did not go into the drug store to buy them, since they were behind the counter and would not be sold to you by some druggists. A good friend, who believed in "safe sex" in those days undoubtedly made purchases for him.

I emulated movie stars; I collected their pictures from the newspaper and created a big scrapbook of articles about them, even enrolling in some fan clubs. I bought the monthly issue of *Modern Screen* [118] with my ten-cent allowance so I could see who was married to whom and who was waiting in the wings. These role models provided me a great fantasy of life beyond Barrett and how the elite lived.

I was fascinated with Rita Hayworth's marriage to the Ala Khan and Joan Crawford's benevolence in adopting two needy children. Alan Ladd always had a new wife and Elizabeth Taylor's marriage was Hollywood-proof, that is, until she eventually became a serial divorcee. I grew up on bad popcorn, worn out theatre seats and double features. In those days, the double feature was one blockbuster movie paired with a run-of-the-mill Western, much like the flip side of recordings, one hit song with another you never wanted. Hollywood churned them out and I saw four or six a week, depending on my brother's love life.

Valley Christian Church in Hood River valley was our church home. It had an active youth program, Christian Endeavor, plus a well-run Sunday School. We were cleaned up and all went to church as a family on Sunday, except for Dad. He rarely attended unless we were in a program. The Mom-Dad tension was reflected in their religious preference for baptism. Dad was sprinkled but Mom was dunked. She believed you could only be saved by full immersion while Dad believed

---

[118] https://en.wikipedia.org/wiki/Modern_Screen

sprinkling was just as good. Dad eventually was dunked in his later years, but not in a baptistery. It occurred in Mosier Creek in the old swimming hole near Dora R.'s. I have no doubt it was colder than a baptistery.

Rev. Lawrence P. was the resident vicar, a portly, jolly man with a hearty laugh and a pompous sermon delivery. He was good to us. He led Bible study at the elementary school, before it was disallowed, probably because of the Supreme Court case, Everson v. Board of Education of Ewing Township in 1947. [119] When the older children had a camp opportunity for a week in Cove, Oregon, which is near La Grande, he loaded his old car with young people and stormed up Cabbage Hill outside of Pendleton. The heavy load and the inadequate radiator always resulted in the old Chevy boiling over.

Camp was $10 per person for a week, which included transportation, lodging, food and Christian education. Our family could not afford it for Tom and Caroline. Ten dollars times two people was a lot of money. One Sunday after church, the day before the group was departing for Cove, Rev. P. arrived to say an anonymous church member had covered the camp fee for both. As usual, Mom burst into tears, Caroline and Tom began packing and I jumped for joy, knowing I was going to be the center of attention without teasing and baiting for a full week. It was a godsend, manna at our feet, and we did eventually learn who had made the contribution. It was Dorothy and Dick R., for whom Caroline baby-sat. They were not rich, just comfortable, but always charitable to us. It was a great experience for both of my siblings, probably more for being away from chores and parents, than epistles and revelations. How grateful my family was for this kindness and generosity.

We were always seeking ways to earn money. Picking fruit in the summer was a natural. Roy H., a senior member of the Valley Christian Church, had a small orchard and we were invited to pick his crop of Royal Ann, Bing and Lambert cherries. He even let Caroline and me (Tom was not involved) have separate picker numbers so our tally would result in our own check at the end of the season. At my age of ten or eleven, I thought the season lasted forever, but it was probably only two or three weeks. The cherries were weighed and our work was tallied. I earned $15 for my work.

I was going to spend it all on candy and toys. "No", said Mom: "Your money will be split three ways. One-third will be for school clothes, one third for savings and one-third for needs and wants throughout the year, given out as you justify those needs." Mom should have been a financial

---

[119] http://www.pewforum.org/files/2007/05/religion-public-schools.pdf

planner. It was an excellent lesson to learn: you don't burn all that you earn. (Although Mom in her youth spent her last 25 cents on stale cashews at Newberry's in Los Angeles, then bagged a job the next morning.) I can still remember the shirts I bought with my $5 for clothes. I think I wore them a little prouder and took better care of them. From that time on, regardless of my financial situation, I was never without a savings account, IRA or 401-K. And I have never been broke in my life.

Incidentally, Roy H. always celebrated the conclusion of the cherry harvest. He hosted a social with homemade ice cream, devil's food cake and a variety of punches and cookies. His huge backyard became a wonderland with outdoor lights. Most of the pickers came from the Valley Christian Church, so it was pretty much a church social as well. It was a wonderful way to conclude the season. I enjoyed functions like that a great deal, although they were not frequent in our experiences. I always remember that prosperous people were generous people as well, giving back to their workers and the community at large. That was a good lesson and I have observed it most of my adult life.

We stayed in the Barrett shack well beyond our needs. Only inertia kept us there, because we had two wage earners contributing to family welfare. Money was there, if not in abundance, at least for what we really needed. For one Christmas, Mom bought a small combination record player and radio from Montgomery Ward. Included were a Looney Tunes [120] record as well as the Perry Como Christmas album.[121] We imitated the voices of Bugs Bunny and Elmer Fudd and learned every song and routine on those albums, which included six big 78-rpm disks, packed in a huge folder.

It was always exciting when the Christmas mail-order catalogs arrived in early November. We were invited to circle what we might want. It was even more exciting when the box actually arrived in the mail in anticipation of Christmas morning. I did receive a train one year. It was not a Lionel electric train set, but had an engine with a wind-up coil that propelled it. A Lionel [122] probably would have blown a fuse, anyway. I loved that train, even though it just went in a circle, never somewhere.

Another year, it was a Tinker Toy set,[123] not an erector set like my friends received. Tom and I had great fun building towers and windmills with those wooden components. He could look at a diagram and guide me into the construction of it, which was probably his incipient

---

[120] https://en.wikipedia.org/wiki/Looney_Tunes
[121] http://www.songfacts.com/detail.php?id=9572
[122] http://www.lionel.com/about/
[123] http://www.knex.com/products/tinkertoy/

construction skill manifesting itself long before he graduated as a civil engineer from Oregon State College in 1960. But, as I said earlier, he got Dad's spatial intelligence.

After the nomadic life during World War II, it was hard to pick up and move, especially with school and church friends. The house was wretched, but our friends never were embarrassed to visit us there. In the winter of 1948, an especially hard one for the Northwest, the west wind blew so hard against the front of the shack that Dad was certain it would topple in. He went to the barn and brought a huge 4 x 6 inside the house, nailing it to the wall as well as the floor. It stayed there all winter and was a great place for hanging clothes to dry. The wall held.

Mom's brother Julius and his spouse, Toots, visited from California one summer. Aunt Toots refused to stay there. She had never experienced a privy, especially one with such an active rat. They never visited us again in that setting and when they did at another house, they had already booked a motel in town. Aunt Toots was never to be denied.

After living in the old house three years, Dad added three bedrooms to the back of the structure. No blueprints, no surveyors, no architect, no building permits. He simply bought the lumber, set up the foundation and began building, much like he had done for the barn he constructed on the property a year earlier. How great it was when he cut the doorway from the old house and we went into the new section. This greatly expanded our living area but it was still pretty rustic. At least the neighbors now knew that we were not all sleeping in the same room, or, as was wagged, the same bed.

My brother graduated high school in 1948 and began to work around the Hood River area, including the Jaymar Lumber Mill. He wanted his own car and found a 1941 Oldsmobile convertible, [124] owned by Ted E., a local rancher. It was a spiffy car but cost $1200. One did not lease a car in those days and installment purchase was pretty well unknown. Dad loaned him the money and the convertible entered our premises. It was tan with a soft beige top and leatherette interior. Mom and Dad never knew, but among the young men of Hood River, it was well known as the "pussy wagon".

In 1950, war broke out in Korea [125] and conscription was once again instituted for young men. Tom registered with the draft board and knew he was going to be called up, since he was not going to college and did not have a strategic job. He joined the Navy, but before it became

---

[124] http://www.arnoldclassiccars.com/5930.html
[125] http://www.history.com/topics/korean-war

official, his draft notice came. Fortunately, the draft board saw the intent and released him from Army duty, which would have sent him into battles on the cold Korean peninsula. How well the Korean Memorial in Washington D.C. portrays what we felt our soldiers were experiencing in Asia.[126] Rather, Tom served at Moffett Field [127] near San Francisco as a radioman for the MATS (Military Air Transport Service) squadron,[128] as well as on the USS Kenneth Whiting, a seaplane tender.[129]

We were distraught when the passenger train took him from Hood River to Portland, and then all the way to San Diego for basic training. This train was definitely going somewhere and so was Tommy. He missed Christmas that year; the first time the family had not been together for a major holiday. But we almost missed Christmas, too, since there was going to be a major move, away from the tumbled-down shack in Rockford.

The first I heard about the move was when I arrived home from sixth grade on a gray December afternoon. Dad was sitting on an orange crate with another man, on the guest crate. I was introduced, just like an adult. We were buying a store in Dallesport, Washington, and this gentleman was from Union 76,[130] the petroleum distributor whose gasoline we would be peddling. Besides a gas station, it included a general store and a short-order kitchen. For me, there would be a new school, new friends and a new state. We were buying the business, including its good will, while renting the building in which all of this occurred.

I was excited, but I would be leaving an unfinished mural for Mary N. at Barrett that had occupied our attention at school, since we had both finished all the sixth grade assignments through the end of May. Mrs. Nora J., my sixth grade teacher, had encouraged students to look into her lesson plan book and work ahead. Since I usually finished my assignments quickly, I worked ahead through the end of the school year. Most teachers allowed quicker students to do a science or art project to fill their time, rather than giving additional homework. I also read over 100 books that year. Most of my teachers probably had a nine-month normal school diploma, not a college degree. But they were good teachers and knew children better than many teachers with advanced

---

[126] http://www.koreanwarvetsmemorial.org/memorial

[127] https://en.wikipedia.org/wiki/Moffett_Federal_Airfield

[128] https://en.wikipedia.org/wiki/List_of_military_squadrons_and_aircraft_based_at_Moffett_Field

[129] https://en.wikipedia.org/wiki/USS_Kenneth_Whiting_(AV-14)

[130] https://en.wikipedia.org/wiki/76_(gas_station)

degrees I later learned to know. And they cared deeply about their students.

With this move, Mother had almost returned to her hometown of Yakima, now less than 100 miles away. My Dad would be his own boss. My brother was pulling bivouac near National City, so he escaped all of this. My poor sister, however, now midway through her senior year, had to finish it in a new high school. A reasonably good student at Hood River High School, when she finished her senior year at Lyle, she would be asked to be valedictorian. No need for Janzen sweaters, Pendleton skirts and Armishaw saddle shoes in Lyle. Jeans and flannel shirts were *de rigueur*. And I was going to finish the sixth grade in a new school in a new state.

Chapter 10 Last Resort: Move To Dallesport

After the Christmas play (we had Christmas plays in public schools in 1950), our neighbors gathered around us as we described our move. The neighborhood had been stable since the war ended. No new families in, no old families out. There were different levels of houses on Markham Lane, some old and some older, but we knew everyone and what they did for a living. If someone's house burned, and that seemed to happen at least once every winter, food and clothing were brought in. We were leaving this safe environment for a new state, a new enterprise, running a combination general store, short-order restaurant and gas station. Would it work? How would our lives be different?

The Dallesport store was exactly across from The Dalles, Oregon, a town of 7600 in 1950.[131] The Dalles was bigger than Hood River and we had always journeyed there when we lived in Hood River for "big" items we could not find in Hood River. This was a great excursion, almost as exciting as our annual trek to Montgomery Wards [132] on Vaughn Street in Portland, where we might even have lunch in the big cafeteria. (We always called it "Monkey Wards") The Dalles had a unique, colorful flavor with the presence of Native Americans along the street, often selling fish or beads. There were stores that sold saddles and other horsey appurtenances. It was a foreign land to me. From Dallesport, which was a pretty lonely spot on Highway 14, we could look across the Columbia River at Mt. Hood during clear days and at night, the bright lights of The Dalles, gleaming like a diminutive "strip" at night.

In January, Mom drove both Caroline and me to the new school in Lyle. My school was a new one-story building with three big classrooms with a whole bank of windows on one side. Caroline's high school was up the hill on the same grounds. It was an old wooden building, a virtual firetrap. I was introduced to my first male classroom teacher, Mr. B., a young man in his 30s, who dressed always in a white shirt and tie with tailored slacks. His shoes always seemed to be shined, even after rain, probably from a weekly session with his Shinola kit. He was nice and I was placed in a classroom of fifth and sixth graders. Everyone looked at me.

These students appeared so different from my classroom at Barrett. Maybe Washingtonians came from a different genetic pool? Some of the boys were really tall and seemed a lot older. The girls were a mixed bag, some with Shirley Temple innocence and others who had generous boobs of great proportion and already knew where, why and when to buy Kotex.

---

[131] https://en.wikipedia.org/wiki/The_Dalles,_Oregon
[132] n.wikipedia.org/wiki/Montgomery_Park_(Portland,_Oregon)

It was a bit bewildering to me. Lyle drew students from a large area, east to Maryhill and north to Beasey Corners. Families represented a mixture of socio-economic levels, some wealthy ranchers, others, day laborers. When all the Bluebird school buses were in port, it looked like the depot of a massive transit system.

Washington's curriculum seemed more advanced than what we studied in Oregon. There was world history and sixth graders were reading about the Mediterranean area and the Rock of "Jaboulder." I had never learned about things outside of the United State but I could list all 48 states and their capitals. I knew every Oregon county and its county seat. I could create a Papier-mâché map of Oregon and place all the hills, valleys and rivers correctly, represented with vivid colors from cans of powdered paint. But what was this Spain and Italy thing?

There was a quiz right after the geographical reading lesson my first day and I missed almost everything. From top of the class and general whiz kid at Barrett, I was now someone who could neither spell Gibraltar nor find it on a map. Would I be sent to Mr. G., the principal? Mrs. G. taught the first and second graders down the hall from my room and they became good friends of our family while we lived there and beyond. They were both instrumental in encouraging me to pursue a career in education.

That evening, when Caroline and I both said we did not want to return to those schools, I learned exactly what that big rock was called. (And when I visited that infamous rock in 1990 and lost my favorite sunglasses, I chuckled over that memory!) I would be taking the school bus that came by the store the next day. Mom could not be spared from the store, what with pumping gas, cooking burgers and overseeing punchboards, where cheating was common.

It took a few days and a few recesses at Lyle Elementary until I caught the flavor. The kids were very friendly, particularly those big guys who must have been retained a few grades to be so tall in the sixth grade. Gordon M. became my champion and buddy, protecting me on the playground. We were the local Lyle version of Mutt and Jeff.[133] It was a different environment, much more worldly than I had experienced in Hood River. The kids knew profanity I had never heard and they used it on the playground. They knew all about sex and would point out a "cock rubber" on the sidewalk if one had been used the night before and discarded by some hot-blooded high school boy.

---

[133] https://en.wikipedia.org/wiki/Mutt_and_Jeff

Mr. B. was a marvel of facilitating both grades. While he taught a lesson to the fifth graders, the sixth graders did their homework, and vice versa. (I had to negotiate the same trick my first year of teaching too!) I can't imagine how he managed his lesson plans, but every teacher I had ever known had a red book with days of the week in it. They wrote assignments down in that. It was basically just "page 45, do questions 1-5 plus 7", but the motivation and instruction came through their personality. If we had a quiz, we exchanged papers to grade them, so marking assignments was minimal.

I never had any bad teachers, at least in my perception. Many of them seemed okay and many were wonderful to me. Had I ended up with a bad one and complained to my parents, it would have been a problem with "me", not them, anyway. My parents totally supported our teachers from the get-go. There was no triangulation with instructors since my parents always took the school's side.

School got better and I played sports at Lyle, particularly since Mr. B. joined us. He provided skill development for boys like me. Softball was the game of choice every recess and I learned to whack pretty well with a bat, even though I was slow in getting to first base and was usually declared "out". I was growing into a chubby six grader. Even at Barrett, Mr. S. had exclaimed, "Look at the big, fat wholloper" as I exited the car at his house. My brother and sister did not help in this destruction of self-concept, teasing I had "carrot legs". Not true. My legs were more like puffy potatoes, achieved by eating too many mashed potatoes, prepared with real cream and butter.

I was never denied food, nor the weekly Mountain Bar, Almond Joy or Butterfinger. It played havoc with both my teeth and my body stature. By the end of the sixth grade, I weighed only ten pounds less than the adult weight I have carried most of my life, 185 pounds. But I was only five-feet tall. No wonder Mom had to buy "husky" jeans for me and then cut eight inches from the hem. Everyone knew "husky" was merely a euphemism for "fat".

Unlike Barrett hot lunches, where you bought a monthly pass that was stamped each day, the hot lunch at Lyle was 15 cents a day, cash only. I was given 75 cents for the week, but sometimes would skip the hot lunch, because it was an open campus. I would go to the Dinner Bell in town and have a hamburger. I'm not certain where I got the money, but I did receive a good allowance for helping in the store at Dallesport. All of this added the pounds and taunting of "fatty", which I lived with through the eighth grade.

In my perception, which has changed little since sixth grade, I always attributed obesity to over-eating and under-moving, not to an emotional situation, glandular disorder or genetics. It may be an unfair bias, but I can't shake it. During my adult life, I have never been overweight, although I would wish my BMI were less than 25. [134] If I live long enough, it will happen as the flesh sloughs away and one becomes a walking skeleton covered by skin. Not soon I hope.

School settled in for me and in a short time I became a class leader in academics once again, asked by Mr. B. to tutor the fifth graders in spare moments. Mr. B. must have seen I was "born to teach". We had a science project, capturing unique insects, bringing them to class, impaling them with a small pin and mounting them in a display case. The "bug" project was huge and we all had to identify the insect we brought in (alas, there were numerous household flies and moths), research its life cycle and write a few paragraphs about it. This was compiled into a book we each were to receive at the end of the year. Caroline, who had consummate typing skills, transferred all the cursive to Pica on duplicator paper, those wretched sheets that turned your fingers purple-blue. I ran these off at the high school. Even now, when I drive through Lyle or see it from the Oregon side on I-84, I wonder if that bug collection is still there. I don't think we adequately preserved the insects so they probably crumbled into dust long before The Dalles Dam [135] was completed and Celilo Falls [136] flooded.

The Native American culture, part of the Yakima tribe,[137] was alive at Dallesport. Their history is magnificently documented at Maryhill Art Museum, twenty miles east of Dallesport on Highway 14.[138] There was a native fishing site close by called Spearfish in Washington or Celilo Falls on the Oregon side.[139] Termed the W'yam people, they were frequent and good customers in our store. During the season when fish were running up the Columbia, money was plentiful but was often spent quickly on new cars or trucks. It was not uncommon for a member of the tribe to stop by the store in a shiny new Bel Air or Chieftain sedan, fresh Chinook salmon marinating in fishy juices on the rear seat or in the trunk.

We often bartered for fresh fish, but my Dad was also generous in extending credit to the First Americans for groceries and gasoline. He

---

[134] http://www.nhlbi.nih.gov/health/educational/lose_wt/BMI/bmicalc.htm
[135] http://www.cbr.washington.edu/hydro/thedalles
[136] https://en.wikipedia.org/wiki/Celilo_Falls
[137] http://www.yakamanation-nsn.gov
[138] http://www.maryhillmuseum.org
[139] http://www.critfc.org/salmon-culture/tribal-salmon-culture/celilo-falls/

kept a hand-ledgered notebook, which listed each account and how much was owed. Not a single person stiffed him over the nine months we spent at Dallesport, except for the few who drove their car over a bluff in the Gorge after too much "fire water" on a Saturday night.

Since the Native economy depended on the sale of fish, which were netted and speared at the Great Falls, a bounty of product and a fast sale would result in a knock on our store door around midnight, long after the store was closed. The borrower wanted to pay his bill before the money was spent on more frivolous goods, which often came in the form of bootlegged, cheap whiskey, since alcohol was denied First Americans by law until 1953. [140] Dad never refused the opportunities for nocturnal visitations when it resulted in a bill being settled. With the same breath, however, the client would probably open a new account and charge a bounty of merchandise once again.

The First People would come in the store, sit on Mrs. R.'s sofa, which was showing the ravages of time by then, much like they did on the street corners of The Dalles. A Coca Cola (and it was not called "coke") might be purchased for a dime. Two hours later, it might be a bottle of Nehi crème soda. After an afternoon of taciturn presence, the car might be filled with gasoline, at 30 cents a gallon for a total bill less than one pays now for an entire gallon. Our visitors would then leave.

I remember sharing my 12th birthday cake that year on March 6 with a Native couple, Calvin and Millie, their two children, one a babe in arms, the other a toddler. It was my idea to invite them. Millie was not more than 16 at the time, but had attended the missionary school at Warm Springs. She had been somewhat Anglo-sized and was comfortable with us. She was also a big flirt and was only four years older than I. Calvin was totally tribal and was not comfortable with us. All enjoyed the cake and ice cream but the banter was constipated. This celebration might have carried the cultural exchange too far. We did go by their shack in Spearfish later for a visit, but did not stay long inside. They informed us there was a rattlesnake somewhere in their bedroom and their native beliefs prevented it from being expelled, dead or alive.

The economy of the Dallesport store depended on the salmon run. When fishing dried up, so did business. Another general store and gas station down the road, owned by Abbey H, was a competitor, but only in a friendly fashion. She had been there for years and the local ranchers preferred the Chevron brand of fuel to our Union 76. They could also fill

---

[140]

http://digitalcommons.unl.edu/cgi/viewcontent.cgi?article=3432&context=greatplainsquarterly

their water tanks there, which Dad resented unless users were spending dollars in our store.

The short order cooking was quite an experience. My mother could deliver a 50-cent hamburger, including potato chips and dill pickles, for only 35 cents. She never made up for it with volume but customers came back again and again. There must have been a half of pound of meat in each. She usually delivered one for me too, which did not help my carrot legs.

There was a little professional soup arrangement behind the bar with a variety of Campbell soups. You opened a can, dropped the contents into a heater and then served it to a customer in a ceramic bowl with handle after it was heated. It cost twenty cents. It was fast food and pretty nutritious, that is, except for its high sodium content. But pity poor Mom running the store solo when Dad was out picking up supplies. She might be cooking a hamburger for several folks at the counter, pumping gas with no hose across the driveway to signal a car and watching someone cheat on the many punchboards we hosted.

Punchboards [141] are a lost art, but they existed in stores like ours for customers to punch through a board, made of heavy cardboard, extract a piece of paper from the backside that had a number on it. Each punch cost a nickel or dime. Certain numbers translated into a prize, mounted on a shelf behind the counter. Sometimes these were wrapped and secret, other times, openly revealed.

It was common for a trickster to hold a finger over part of the number to claim a prize. That happened to Mom several times and made Dad furious when he returned from hunting and gathering. Such cheating rendered the future of that particular board useless. Other gamers would calculate how many punches remained on a board, weigh it against what objects were yet to be garnered and then buy out the board. Most board prizes were simply carnival junk but some customers wanted to win, regardless of the prize. And it satisfied people's gaming urges long before casinos and lotteries.

While we were at Dallesport, Tom came home for a brief furlough after Naval basic training in San Diego. He always had a host of friends with him, mostly from Hood River days, and was never home much. He demonstrated marching maneuvers to us in the front of the store. We were relieved to learn he was going to be stationed near San Francisco at Moffett Field. He would re-claim his Oldsmobile convertible for this billeting since he would be stateside.

---

[141] https://en.wikipedia.org/wiki/Punchboard

Only later would he ship out for almost a year on the USS Kenneth Whiting, which would lead him into war waters. This assignment qualified him for the GI Bill of Rights,[142] when he was honorably discharged. This would ultimately help finance him through Oregon State College as well as provide low mortgage rates for his first home. It was a wise Congress and President that instituted the GI Bill, enabling men from a lower-economic status to aspire to a college degree and home ownership. This was a small repayment for sacrificed years in the military fighting a war that someone else had started. It also pumped up the American economy and enhanced the educational level of the national workforce, long after World War II and the Korean conflict had passed.

Caroline's social life was varied and risky at the store. Lyle High School was a breeze for her so she would hitchhike home or go across the river to Hood River to see old friends, with whom she should have been graduating. A local car dealer and family acquaintance, Ed R., offered her a ride and lectured her on the value of education. But she was pretty and fun. Boys were attracted to her for all the right reasons as well as other reasons best attempted but not achieved in the backseat of an old Buick. Even the older men were attracted to her, including Bill S., a lonely local, who brought her sheet music and chocolates for playing the piano for him.

Guys from high school and the area would come into the store, buy something to eat at the counter and play a little pinball on our Bally.[143] She would grace them with her presence, usually in a tight pullover sweater that pushed her boobs into presentation position. If the sweater were not working, she would disappear into the residential part of the store and change it, reappearing so those breasts were not missed. It worked. She had lots of dates and Dad never knew where she was. She would simply disappear for hours in the evening, long after the store closed.

One night, she and her love of the moment pulled up in front of the store, totally dark now at 2 a.m. A good night kiss was in the works. Dad hit the neon Union 76 sign switch, which illuminated all of Dallesport. She quickly exited that car as the young stud spun gravel in his Ford coupe to escape Dad's wrath.

Clyde K. was a particular paramour, son of Horse Thief K. Papa and Clyde would round-up wild horses, which roamed the puffy hills of the

---

[142] http://www.benefits.va.gov/gibill/history.asp
[143] https://en.wikipedia.org/wiki/Bally_Manufacturing

Columbia Gorge east of The Dalles, and sell them to a glue factory. Clyde was divorced and very handsome. Caroline was immediately attracted to him and went with him on these horse-round-ups.

We thought she would drop out of high school and marry him, but she did not. He looked much like Elvis Presley, a bit earlier than we knew of Elvis, and much earlier than all the clones his music and persona birthed. Caroline graduated from Lyle High School in the spring of 1951, but not as valedictorian. She refused the honor and deferred to another girl who had attended high school there for a longer time. Although the class was small, the celebration was still profound.

For a brief time, Dad drove the Dallesport school bus route to earn extra money. The store was not a cash cow and supplies were expensive. Mom's hamburgers did not help. There was little profit in gasoline, possibly one or two cents a gallon. Native Americans were loyal customers, when they had money, which was only during the salmon run. Abby's, down the road, had a liquor license. She could set up Olympia and Rainier stubbies for construction workers, who were beginning to flood the area, what with the prospect of a new dam as well as a new bridge being constructed in the area.

Now, with my seventh grade status during the summer vacation of 1951, I helped in the store. Mostly it was tending the gas pumps, which had two grades of gas, regular and ethyl. There was no gasoline grade termed "unleaded". Big cars required ethyl, older ones, only regular, all of it leaded. I was puzzled when I first tried to fuel a 1950 Fleetwood.[144] There was no gas cap. Where could it be? General Motors had crafted it into one of the enormous fins in back. You pushed the reflector light underneath and the fin popped up. Hidden inside was the gas cap.

Credit cards [145] were used, but rarely. The card was a plastic device with the owner's name, but no magnetic strip. The information had to be written by hand on a special receipt, including the owner's name, the card number, the gallons and the price. A duplicate copy went to the purchaser, the rest in a special box in the National Cash Register,[146] which would pop up a series of tabs showing the dollars, the tens and the cents. When the Union 76 tanker delivered gas, the receipts were exchanged for the delivery. It was usually tick for tack. There was little profit in selling gasoline but it got customers into the stores to buy a soda, savor a hamburger and play the jukebox or pin ball machine, much like Quick Marts and Seven-Elevens of today. The register held all

---

[144] https://www.hagerty.com/price-guide/1950-Cadillac-Fleetwood_Series_75
[145] http://www.creditcards.com/credit-card-news/credit-cards-history-1264.php
[146] http://www.collectorsweekly.com/coin-operated/cash-registers

of our cash as well, which was the primary way to exchange dollars for goods and services. There were few checks and fewer credit cards.

Our little store, which seemed big to me at the time, was a mixture of business and residence. The back area was residential but we had to use the store bathrooms in front, should the urge emerge. The shower and laundry building was separate from the store. There was no store kitchen for the preparation of short orders. This was accomplished in our own kitchen, using our household plates. There was no dishwasher, except for Caroline and me. Hours would pass without a customer and we grew bored leaning on our elbows, standing behind the serving counter and waiting. We ate lots of the profits, too, but lived well. I was fat but everyone else in the family looked well fed too. We kept pets, which roamed freely. Our house cats soon became hors d'oeuvres for the local coyotes. We were devastated when Husky, Tom's little dog, was hit and killed by a passing car on busy Highway 14. Happy, the mother fox terrier, survived.

In those down times, Mom or Dad would take me to the ferry head about two miles from the store. I would buy a ten-cent ferry [147] pass as a walk-on-traveler and cross the Columbia River to The Dalles. At either the Granada [148] or the Columbia ,[149] I could escape to the land of cowboys, space travelers or pirates through flickering images on a silver screen. Other times, Dad would simply close the store. We would take a picnic and fishing poles to one of the mountain lakes south of Hood River, where it was cooler and the wind did not blow. Upon return, there would always be a note from an angry customer who needed gas but was deferred because we had closed for the afternoon. They probably filled up at Abby's and enjoyed an Olympia beer as well.

It was a lonely life and not one to which Dad had aspired. He was not customer-oriented and somehow never accepted that the customer is always right. He felt the operative adverb was "sometimes", not "always". Mom was lonely and missed her garden and close church friends. Even though we were in Washington, it was not Yakima. We could hear the trains on the Washington tracks near the river. The SP&S line[150] was built in the early 1900s by Sam Hill, the same man who built Maryhill Museum.[151] He wanted a rail line that would compete with Oregon's Union Pacific. All those trains, both sides of the Columbia River, went somewhere, and we all wondered where.

---

[147] http://historichoodriver.com/index.php?showimage=1094
[148] https://en.wikipedia.org/wiki/Granada_Theater_(The_Dalles,_Oregon)
[149] http://cinematreasures.org/theaters/37205
[150] http://columbiariverimages.com/Regions/Places/washington_tunnels.html
[151] http://www.maryhillmuseum.org

The wind never stopped. We were on the cusp of the air pressure differential between east and west, wind blowing through the narrow Columbia Gorge, which acts like a wind tunnel. I never knew people combed their hair until I was in college in Portland. After nine months struggling to make a profit, the store went on the market and sold in August 1951. We would move to Mosier, a village between The Dalles and Hood River, and buy a house. Dad would return to Jaymar Lumber Mills for employment. He wanted someone else to be the boss. Mom would return to her friends at the packing sheds for seasonal work in the fall. And I would begin the seventh grade at Mosier School.

Chapter 11 On Mosier, On Mosier

The building looked like Leavenworth Federal Penitentiary [152] and the fight song to the tune of "On Wisconsin" [153] expounded:

"On, Mosier, On, Mosier,
This is our war cry.
Keep the good old school before you,
Never it let it die.

On Mosier, On, Mosier,
Fight on for your fame,
Fight, Mosier, fight, fight, fight,
We'll win this game!"

I sang that song for the next six years, until I graduated from its hallowed halls, but never understood the "fame" part of the lyrics. We won some games and lost some. We competed with Lyle, Arlington, Moro, Dufur, Cascade Locks and Heppner, all small rural schools. No state championships, to be certain. No athletic scholarships to university teams. So the fame was wishful thinking, not reality. I'm not certain the "war cry" was justifiable, either. We were generally pretty peaceful.

Mosier [154] is a small bedroom community that had a population of 259 in 1950, so we helped it grow when we moved there in August of 1951. It lies on the south side of the Columbia in an expansive bend of the river, closer to Hood River on the west than The Dalles on the east. Its beauty is unspeakable, only surpassed by its omnipresent wind. Highway 30, now a scenic bypass,[155] was the only road going into town, but it did exit on the other side for those who wanted to pass through. I was among those who would have preferred to pass through my first few weeks there.

I reluctantly moved from Lyle. I had status working in the store and plenty of cash and candy, the latter of which I purloined regularly from Dad's inventory. My sister was more generous in her larceny, taking a bite out of a candy bar, replacing its wrapper and returning it to the shelf. I wonder how many customers headed west on Highway 14 in their shiny post-war Rocket 88 Oldsmobiles ,[156] unwrapped their candy

---

[152] https://www.bop.gov/locations/institutions/lvn/
[153] https://en.wikipedia.org/wiki/On,_Wisconsin!
[154] https://en.wikipedia.org/wiki/Mosier,_Oregon
[155] http://columbiariverimages.com/Regions/Places/mosier.html
[156] http://www.boldride.com/ride/1951/oldsmobile-88/image/5

bar and exclaimed: "What is this? Someone took a bite out of this candy bar."

Our Mosier place was purchased from Mr. and Mrs. G., older folks, who wanted us to buy their furniture too. We did not want it and that set up a barrier immediately. The house was old and had been added on without any architectural finesse. It was not structurally sound, particularly the master and only bedroom, which sat on dirt, not a foundation. The basement was cold and creepy, with floor joist above that moved if one walked across the living room. There were large scorpions lurking there. There was no furnace, just a circulating oil heater in the living room for heat. Our well-traveled wood range was installed in the kitchen for cooking and heating water.

The Mosier property consisted of .9 acres on Highway 30, a quarter mile east of Mosier itself. The Union Pacific track, with a siding, was below the house. There was constant noise, whistles and wheezes from passing trains, both passenger and freight. I would watch and listen to the trains, wondering where all those well-dressed travelers in the club cars were going. I realized a train, bus or car would someday take me out of this town. I became so conditioned to train sounds that I could sleep beside a track even now and never hear them.

Highway 30 going east climbed slightly out of Mosier, so our house was where every large vehicle shifted down slightly, if east-bound for The Dalles, or engaged an exhaust brake, if west-bound for Hood River. There was a lot of noise from backfiring and double clutching.

There was a large lawn with big oak and maple trees, which would produce a surfeit of leaves in October that I would rake. There were a few fruit trees, Lambert and Royal Ann cherries, plus a small Italian prune tree. There was a large garden plot, which was an attraction for Mom. She believed that if one owned property and paid taxes, one should harvest a return from the land, whether fruit, vegetables or hay.

The house was small with a built-on glass porch where I would have a bed and with extra space for a washing machine. There were also two huge sinks for washing produce, hairy dogs or muddy feet. There was a chicken barn of considerable size as well as a small cabin a distance from the house, which had been a work shed. It would become a bedroom for Caroline. In the main house, there was one small bathroom with a claw-footed tub.

Most of the house had been glitzed up with wallpaper of dubious taste to garner a sale. The outside had asphalt brick siding that covered the rough boards that made up the walls, not much different from the rough exterior of the Rockford shack. The attic, which had a space for accessing, was devoid of all insulation. Dad paid cash for the property, $5700 and we moved in mid-August 1951. Mom and Dad would stay on the property until their deaths; hers in 1987, his 1999, 40 days shy of the new century. They would build a new house next door, however, and live in it from 1975 on.

Consumer goods were being produced by the burgeoning American economy by 1951 and we had money to purchase them. Household income was growing, whether measured in actual dollars or dollars adjusted for time and inflation.[157] Eventually, the wood stove was replaced with a Hotpoint electric push-button range with four burners, the old water heater with an electric model and the fridge with a new GE sans the clock in the door. It had a regular freezer on top, small, but better than the old Norge. It even kept ice cream hard. We made a trip to Vaughn Street in Portland and bought a sofa, chair, two end tables and a coffee table, plus a Formica kitchen table with four chairs covered with matching red plastic. This was the post-war modern look.

Soon after the move, we purchased a new automobile. I had hoped for a red Buick Roadmaster[158] with a Dynaflow transmission, but that was beyond the needs or financial ability of our family. It turned out to be a GMC ¾ ton pickup.[159] But it was red and it was new. Pickups in those days were utility vehicles, not showy transportation or status symbols like a Silverado, F-150 or Ridgeline.

Dad had a good job as a tallyman and carrier driver at Jaymar Lumber Mill at first and then Stevenson-Daubenspeck-Stevenson[160] in Bingen, Washington, when Jaymar folded. SDS, as it was known, was a non-union mill, that intended to stay that way by careful attention to its employees. The management established a retirement fund for each worker, much like a 401K, funded entirely by the company. Dad had a nice nest egg when he retired years later.

Mom worked in the fall at the packing shed in Hood River, sometimes in an extended season that went well beyond Christmas. By now, the packing industry had moved to cardboard crates and shrink packs, since the market had become international. With the seniority she had achieved, she could work throughout the year as much as she wanted. Fruit was put into cold storage until it was ready to be packed and

---

[157] http://web.stanford.edu/class/polisci120a/immigration/Median%20Household%20Income.pdf
[158] https://en.wikipedia.org/wiki/Buick_Roadmaster
[159] http://1952gmcpickuptruck.com/description/
[160] http://sdslumber.com

shipped, unlike the old days when it was picked, packed and shipped during the fall harvest. Distribution of goods was changing. In addition, Mom was building a retirement fund for herself, thanks to the vision of the governing union, the Teamsters. [161]

Caroline was slinging hash at various restaurants in The Dalles after graduation, sometimes living at home, other times in a rented room. When Tom arrived home on furlough, he was driving a 1948 Plymouth coupe. Caroline decided she would accompany him back to the San Francisco area, get a job there and be around when he had shore liberty.

A racy lady, not of the night but she could have been, however, accompanied them back to California. She was from the Rockford area in Hood River, married to one of our neighbor's son. Tom probably knew her from high school and then met her in a bar again while on leave. Caroline recalls how this woman left her tiny baby in the house she shared with the husband she was leaving and went to California. The baby would have been alone, unattended, for two hours before her husband returned from work. Caroline roomed with this woman in California for a short while, but the promiscuity was too much. Caroline moved out and soon rented her own apartment. Eventually, she was hired by AT&T and trained as a long-distance telephone operator in Oakland. Tom was shipped out for a nine-month tour on a naval seaplane tender.

But for me, school was a mixed bag. Lyle was a competitor of Mosier and there was spirited animosity at any game between the two rivals, often culminating in fisticuffs outside the locker rooms. Dale W. was the homeroom teacher and seventh grade was considered junior high. We were to rotate for each subject with a different room and a different teacher. This was all new to me and totally frustrating. Where would I keep my books? Why could I not have one of those desks attached in a row? As it turned out, we were assigned lockers.

Every hour, it was a different teacher and a different classroom. The possibilities at Mosier were not limitless. We shuttled back and forth between two or three rooms, including the Industrial Arts room, better known as "Shop". Girls took "Home Economics" while boys did "Shop". I fell into the routine very quickly and eventually liked it. It felt grown up.

My fellow classmates were hostile, even resentful. There were six kids in the seventh grade who had begun first grade together and were still together. It was a coalition, a rat pack, and I was an intruder and new. Furthermore, I was from Lyle and I was fat. June P. and Jan L.

---

[161] https://en.wikipedia.org/wiki/International_Brotherhood_of_Teamsters

immediately called me "Mousey" and took delight in locking me in the storage room every chance they got. Mosier kids were the offspring of a lineage that went back several generations. Everyone knew everyone and everyone was related to everyone else, or so it seemed. This is really not far from the truth. This hostile group proved to become lifelong friends in the next years and I still exchange greetings on Facebook with many. But in the seventh grade, I resented them and they resented me. Mosier continues to be a network of families of close-knit relatives,[162] where you live all of your life, if you can. If you cannot, then you return when you retire. Not for me. It's far too windy.

Homeroom with Dale W., and then English with Miss B, followed by math with someone else and back to Dale W. for social studies. Mr. W. was a nice man who dressed in grey flannels and shiny shoes. Like most teachers, he did not teach, but merely let the textbooks dictate the lessons. In the 1940s and 1950s, it was Scott Foresman, Ginn and Co., and McGraw-Hill who were the teachers. The person in the classroom merely selected the page from their texts as well as the questions to answer. The resident person-in-charge also had a teacher's manual with all the answers. Somehow, native curiosity got many of us through the system and eventually into college, where critical thinking was prime. I didn't mind doing the lessons but I remember being summoned to the principal's office and being reprimanded because I said: "He doesn't teach. We just read what he assigns." I was kicked out of the office and threatened with repercussions if I did not shape up. I never relayed the encounter to my parents. We read on.

In the eighth grade, during my second year at Mosier, there were six boys and six girls. This created a polarity on what was to be done if there were assignments or projects, based entirely on gender. Once, it was proposed we be given math assignments for the entire week so we could work ahead. Unbeknownst to me, the girls all wanted this arrangement. The boys did not, because Mr. W. might forget to do math one day and we would end up with fewer assignments that week. The weekly assignment meant more work and closer accountability.

We voted by show of hands, and I voted with the girls, throwing the election to the weekly commitment. That was the new order and the boys whispered: "We'll get you" for this. As first period ended and we moved on to second, which was Shop, I went to the boys' lavatory and cried. Within ten minutes, Mr. W. came to fetch me and said it was all settled. He had given the boys a little lecture on democracy and voting, not as a block, but as an individual believed. I was greeted by the five fellows and slapped on the back as a hero when I returned to the Shop

---

[162] https://www.facebook.com/www.MosierHistoricalPhotos

room. I had lots of help measuring my boards and sanding my magazine holder project that day. I wish Mr. W were still around to lecture our Congress on this same principle, which might get our country moving forward again without government gridlock. Also, as a compassionate and understanding teacher, he redeemed himself in my mind. And I learned to express and vote my conviction, not follow the crowd.

Some teachers, however, were truly excellent. Mrs. S. could bring *Beowulf* [163] alive by reading it in Old English. Mrs. R. would make us debate Supreme Court decisions or track a law from committee to acceptance in Congress or take the role of one of the signers of the Declaration of Independence, costumes added by participants for effect. But these gems were an anomaly in the entire system. Most teachers were page-assigners, not motivators who instilled a love of learning.

There is a good reason for that. Primarily, these folks were all overworked. They taught seven periods a day, often to a group, which required two streams of instruction within the same class period. They had no prep period. There was no union. They were underpaid, all earning the same salary, regardless of experience or advanced degrees. They coached after school or directed plays in addition to pulling hall or bus duty every few weeks. They took sick kids home or to the doctor in their own cars. And they answered to a school board that wanted miracles, not instruction, and probably thought every teacher was overpaid.

Mosier had some teachers who remained for years, others who passed through and left after a few months. If they were single, they had little social life and, if they did, were scrutinized by a judgmental community. They lived in a town where available housing was sketchy and inadequate. Their cars were old, if they had one. There were no incentives to seek advance education, other than their own personal motivation. Some came but some went.

Nonetheless, I came out of Mosier writing very well. Mrs. S. and Mrs. R. required good writing from all students. We diagrammed expressions [164] until we could visualize what was going on in the language, whether simple, compound or complex sentences. We outlined before we wrote and used a dictionary to find appropriate word usage. We wrote research papers with footnotes and bibliography. We presented oral reports from articles we read in the *Readers' Digest*, [165] a monthly publication. I sailed through college writing with few glitches and have used writing

---

[163] https://en.wikipedia.org/wiki/Beowulf
[164] http://www.wikihow.com/Diagram-Sentences
[165] https://en.wikipedia.org/wiki/Reader%27s_Digest

throughout my entire life and career as a result of that early training. I eventually penned over twelve books, some with national publishers, and earned some awesome royalties at times. Equally important, I still love to write.

Conversely and totally lacking, however, was a basic scientific curriculum, like chemistry, physics and geology. And what a goldmine the Columbia Gorge would have been for the latter subject. We learned biology from a book. There was only one microscope in the entire school and it was probably obtained as a prize from the bottom of a box of Cracker Jacks. And it was particularly disappointing that we skipped Chapter 24 in the book, the only subject which interested us: human reproduction. Consequently, few graduates pursued a career in science and no Mosier graduate ever became an M.D. of which I am aware.

So as to not overburden teachers in the high school, ninth grade English and Literature were taught to the ninth grade one period, the tenth grade the next. This was true for World History. Both ninth and tenth graders got it. The next year, something else in the language arts and social sciences would be offered. If one grade were considered a bit more intelligent than another (and I'm not certain who determined this), they would get a double-whammy for their instruction. Brighter students in the slower class might be bumped up to the next grade for just that class. Thus, it was not surprising to have Modern Problems, a senior course taught to the entire senior class plus the addition of two "brighter" juniors. I don't know how the administration managed it, but they did.

Literature was varied and exciting. We studied the poetry of Keats and Shelly, Wordsworth and Burns. We read the short stories of O. Henry and Guy de Maupassant. One year, we read the libretto of *The Mikado* and then listened to the operetta on 45-rpm discs, those little discs with a big hole in the middle. I even borrowed the album from Mrs. S. and listened at home. I couldn't get enough of *Three Little Maids From School* and *A Wandering Minstrel, I*.[166]

There were boy-girl things. If you had a girl friend, it meant hanging out together in the gym during the noon hour, possibly holding hands (no embraces allowed) and kind of walking in each other's shadow. If you were in high school, it might mean the girl wore her guy's letterman sweater. There might even be a class ring on a chain, hanging from her neck. You would close-dance together, almost exclusively, at the dances after the basketball games. If you were older and had a car, you went to the movies, followed by hamburgers, potato chips and a dill pickle at

---

[166] https://en.wikipedia.org/wiki/The_Mikado

Pop's Place in Hood River or Johnny's Café in The Dalles. There was lots of necking and petting, much like *The Last Picture Show*, [167] but I don't recall any boy was lucky enough to have a Ruth Popper on the side. There could have been sex, too, but it must have been very safe or very virtual, because few turned up pregnant.

There were sports. This generally meant the "coach" threw out a ball and we played without tutelage for an hour. If you wanted to learn the sport, you looked to an older guy who was good to help you. There was basketball for seventh and eighth grade, but no football, no baseball. We had games with other schools, usually in the afternoon. It would have been nice had if there had been track, soccer, Lacrosse, volleyball, badminton, pickleball or rugby. I never thought of myself as an athlete. You could not do music well and be an athlete. Those who were good at the limited sports must have had a father or older brother who pitched to them or threw grounders. I have never even owned a baseball mitt my entire life.

Finally in my mid-seventies on the pickleball court, my playing partners say I'm a good athlete. I have the speed, reflexes and hand-eye coordination that athleticism requires. My perception of self might have been different if someone had made that observation at Barrett, Lyle or Mosier School. And I could have taken remedial science courses in college had I been serious about majoring in science or becoming an M.D. We allow ourselves to adopt self-appointed labels and excuses but we might have overcome any or all of these, had we been so motivated.

In high school, I was the manager of the basketball team as a freshman and a cheerleader my sophomore year. My junior year, I played on the JV basketball squad. Once before half time, knowing the clock was running down, I pitched the ball from mid-court and it went through the hoop. No big deal, just luck. And in those days, it was worth only two points, not three. My senior year, I worked part time and did not participate in sports because I had an accordion studio. I also commuted to Portland on the Greyhound bus for accordion lessons every other Friday.

How did I come to be a cheerleader in a town where boys played sports and girls cheered them on? I came to the sophomore year and was told by Linda K. and Glenna G. that the third member of the rally squad had dropped out of school to become a mother. There was a possibility she would become a wife as well. Rather than take in another person they disliked, who was waiting in the wings, they asked me to audition. Me? A cheerleader?

---

[167] http://www.imdb.com/title/tt0067328/

I had grown out of my middle school fat and had a reasonably good body. I had energy but this was unheard of in Mosier. Of course, we worked out and I auditioned in front of the entire student body, which was only fifty students. I got the position, hands down. It was unanimous. It was an exciting experience because no one in our league had a male cheerleader. We wore white sweaters with block M's attached, white bottoms plus white bucks, and carried maroon megaphones. We were automatically a fearsome trio of energy. These two are still good friends and we still email retorts and in-jokes we used with each other in the 1950s.

I particularly loved autumn at school. There were new clothes with new smells, new books that had not been used before. Fall was the annual Halloween carnival, where the student body transformed the gymnasium into booths with games, prizes and food. It brought out the entire town and it meant reduced classroom involvement for the weeks leading up to it. We always sold apple cider, crafted at Fern W.'s big ranch.

Fern was a well-educated lady, one of the early women graduates from Oregon State College with a master's degree in the 1930s. She managed a large cherry farm but taught business courses at Mosier as well. Each fall, we would press cider at her ranch and have a festive party. The cider was good but lots of boys let it sit for a few days, hoping it would ferment and give them an alcohol high. It resulted in more diarrhea than inebriation, I am certain. But it was an annual tradition.

I always had a love affair with cars, especially at that time of my life. I could not wait to be 15 to obtain a learner's permit. I learned to drive on the old Studebaker sedan, which was pretty battered by now. I was not very good at driving but managed to navigate the back roads of Mosier without landing in the ditch. I went for my practical driver's test on my sixteenth birthday and failed it flat. I did not have enough experience driving in town, so said the examiner. And there had been no driver's training in Mosier High School. I had to wait a month to re-take it and then passed it without problem. That month between, however, seemed more like a year. The only rite of passage we really had in Mosier was the driver's license.

My sister returned from Oakland one fall and took a job with the telephone company in The Dalles. She bought a 1941 Chevrolet coupe[168]

---

[168] https://www.google.com/search?q=1941+Chevrolet+coupe&client=safari&rls=en&tbm=isch&tbo=u&source=univ&sa=X&ved=0CB0QsARqFQoTCKiumavqi8kCFRRGYwodWGUBRg&biw=1302&bih=1002

and used it for commuting. Whatever she paid for it, she more than doubled in repairs at Claude B.'s local garage. Dad did some rebuilding, but the car was old and the engine shot. Although it was never a good car, I eventually inherited it, paying my sister $75 for my half. The joke in the school was it got 20 miles on a gallon of gas and a quart of oil. Eventually, I bought a 1949 Chevrolet sedan, which lasted me through college.

The attitudes we carry through life often come from an early experience that is totally inaccurate. In my retirement years, I have come to believe you can do almost anything if you are exposed to it and are encouraged to enjoy it, whether music, math, pickleball, chess or Sudoku. You may not be a world champion, but you can be adequate. I had to teach math early in my career and found out I had a good aptitude for numbers, which I had denied in high school and college. I know now I could have been a CPA or CFO. Thus, I have no sympathy for those who say "I'm tone deaf", "I have two left feet" or "I was never good at math." We are a product of our environment and our own attitudes. The richer our environment and the more accepting our attitude, the more skills and talents we develop. So much for my view of the Nature-Nurture dichotomy.[169]

The high school was on one side of the Mosier School building, the junior high and elementary grades on the other. In the seventh grade, I had lots of friends in high places. During the noon hour, we would eat our dry peanut butter sandwiches and Red Delicious apples in the home economics room, seated at long, foldable tables. I'll never know why two of the senior girls, both beauties, would always sit with me. I never felt they were laughing at me but perhaps they enjoyed playful banter from one so young. Glade H., who would become my sister-in-law in five more years and her cousin, June H., were nice companions and soul mates. I think we talked about lots of things, probably politics and movie stars, but possibly clothes and music. There were lots of laughs and I had status with my peers because of my association with these older students.

The idyllic nature of Mosier changed my fourth year at Mosier, which was my sophomore grade. We returned in the fall to a school that had doubled in size. There was a construction boom triggered by the construction of The Dalles Dam and an accompanying bridge across the Columbia River below it. This brought numerous new families who followed construction to our area.

---

[169] http://www.simplypsychology.org/naturevsnurture.html

Housing was scarce in Mosier. There had probably been only one new house built in 20 years. An old deserted school on the hill was converted into apartments. People rented their basements and a trailer city sprang up near the high school. Abandoned farms in the hinterlands were suddenly inhabited.

These kids were different. They had moved schools many times in their young lives, following their families to the next site. They were a mixture of half-brothers and stepsisters. These were not "Dick and Jane" families. They were not well schooled because of the moves. Lots of instruction became remedial. Their attitude to the community and their teachers left much to be desired. We had never seen our teachers disrespected before. Petty crime and vandalism began to occur in pristine Mosier.

The impact on the school was severe. The gymnasium was converted into several classrooms, divided by thin partitions. The activity room was divided in half to accommodate the explosion. New teachers were hired, when possible, and older teachers were maxed out with class sizes beyond the optimal. I have always wondered how the school administration dealt with this situation because the newcomers were not contributing to the tax base, as renters and part-time residents. Perhaps emergency funds were available from the state or federal level, since the Federal government funded the construction boom in the area. It was an explosive but exciting time for a small community.

Overnight, the dynamic of the school changed. Attitudes and language we had learned to accept in a small town suddenly were expanded with street words and reactions we had never experienced. Fights in the hall had never happened before. Boy-girl pairings were interrupted with "new meat" on the block, who knew new ways of doing things, especially on the dance floor. I had never heard of the "dirty boogie" until that year. And the lexicon of profanity on the playground expanded geometrically.

This injection of a new demographic was certainly not experienced only in Mosier. It happened wherever new types of people migrated to new regions and upset the status quo. It continues still and is endemic to all societies, whether from construction, natural disasters like tornados, earthquakes, floods or even immigration. "The only thing we can't change is change itself." [170] Little Mosier was shocked out of its prim and self-serving complacency in the fall of 1954. It has never been the same since, even now in its 21st Century attempts at gentrification.[171]

---

[170] http://www.thedailyphilosopher.org/daily/000011.php
[171] http://www.pbs.org/pov/flagwars/special_gentrification.php

In my junior year, my brother married Glada H., my former lunch partner, in a large ceremony at Mosier Christian Church, where both families attended. He had been engaged to Maxine G. before that and we also were certain he was going to wed Jo Evelyn C., at one time. Glada became his spouse of 46 years, through college, through a job at Texaco for most of his career, and then in retirement in Las Vegas.

I was best man for the wedding, a responsibility that included delivering the white dinner jackets back to the rental agency in Portland following the ceremony. After the honeymoon, they lived in a house trailer behind the Mosier School until classes resumed at Portland State. He had four more years of college. He made it through with a degree in civil engineering, thanks to the G.I. Bill and financial support from both sets of parents, Dad and Mom as well as Sterling and Minnie H. His was the first college degree in both families.

There are numerous stories to relay about my time in Mosier. I had lots of friends. I had good and not-so-good teachers. I was involved with the church, particularly serving as a leader in Christian Endeavor. I sang in a quartet and attended three state C.E. conferences. I had girl friends, as one would expect, but there was nothing serious. It meant someone to exchange notes with in class, to tease, to dance with, even to sit with on the school bus to games or to hang out with in the hall during the noon hour. Some classmates did find true love, married and are still together. I was not ready for that. It took me twelve or more years until I was past 30 to find true love.

Many of these stories are best left untold for fear of boring the reader with too much detail when the crux, a word I learned from Mrs. R., of my life has already been conveyed sufficiently. That is, except for my musical education, which came to fruition in Mosier.

Chapter 12   Dilettante With Many Instruments

It's been said, and I don't have the source, a child's musical education should begin 30 years before he or she is born. This is simply a way of saying musical kids come from musical homes.[172] But it is probably also true that mathematicians come from homes where the checkbook is balanced and brain surgeons usually have one parent, if not two, who is an M.D. Teachers beget teachers, dancers, dancers, and so on.

My mother was very musical. She learned the piano as a young child. Her father bought a piano for her in Bend, which, alas, was destroyed in the fire that took their house. She often described seeing that old upright burn, the glues and resins melting and pushing the fireball into greater intensity. Somehow, that love of music and piano playing continued all of her life. Our family did have a piano from 1937, the old Ludwig that was put on the truck with all our earthly possessions and driven from California to Oregon campgrounds. In 1987, 50 years later, it was left to me. Eventually, I passed it on to a family in Pine, Arizona, who had a child interested in music.

Mom was often the church pianist. She was considered the piano teacher of choice in Mosier and she taught each of her kids to play the instrument, as she had promised Dad when the piano was purchased at great sacrifice. Caroline and Tom went through the pedagogy of John Thompson [173] long before I was old enough, but I must have started at age six or seven. Mom was strict. Hands had to be in the right position and whole notes received four counts, not three and a half. You did not speed up nor did you slow down, whether the passage was easy or difficult. I can't say I particularly enjoyed learning from my mother, but I did go through several of the books and learned to read music, both bass and treble clef.

It was more fun to listen to Caroline's improvisations. I would try to imitate her. She would teach me complicated songs by rote and I could play an impressive rendition of *Mona Lisa* and *Dreamer's Holiday* in the fourth grade. In reality, the combination of Caroline's rote-instruction and Mom's note-teaching was totally compatible with contemporary pedagogical practices in musicianship, such as the Suzuki [174] or Orff [175] approaches. Good teachers have been doing this for ages. It's how we learn our native language, that is, you speak before you read. Thus,

---

[172] http://www.pbs.org/parents/education/music-arts/creating-a-musical-home-environment/
[173] http://www.methodbooks.com/store/john-thompson/index.htm
[174] https://suzukiassociation.org/about/suzuki-method/
[175] http://musiced.about.com/od/lessonplans/tp/orffmethod.htm

early in my musical training, I could read music, never as well as I would have liked, and could play by ear, never being afraid to sit down at a keyboard and play without a book in front of me.

With the move to Mosier in 1951, there was a real music program at the school. Mrs. S. had an orchestra, which consisted of violins, baritones, guitars, accordions and ukuleles. Whatever you had or played, Mrs. S. would work you in. The junior high and high school were invited to be part of the ensemble. She always pushed me to try a real instrument, because I was thinking of becoming a world-class ukulele player long before the advent of Tiny Tim. Then I tried the baritone horn (euphonium) and it was a good fit. From then on, I played a variety of brass instruments, including trumpet, trombone and Sousaphone.

Between my seventh and eighth grade, however, Joe P. and Co. from Portland came to town. Joe was an accordion entrepreneur. The accordion was popular in America largely due to Dick Contino, a national virtuoso,[176] who was frequently heard on the Ed Sullivan variety show. Joe brought his own virtuoso performer, Al D., who demonstrated the instrument to the entire school. Who might be interested? Almost everyone. But as it turned out, not everyone turned up for lessons. One would be provided a loaner 12-bass accordion and lessons for $10 a month. This would include group lessons and all the sheet music one needed. I signed up along with many others.

Al was a good teacher, but I was soon bored with the beginners' group. I read music and was musical. Al decided he would provide individual lessons to me after all the groups were done, if I would hang around and help. I did. Then he would drive me home in his 1951 tan Ford Victoria. He would wish my parents well, as dinner was cooking. "Would you like to stay for dinner?" Mom would proffer. He never refused and we were always graced with a concert after dinner, with nice jazz styling. Even my father liked Al. My sister was often there and he was quite attracted to her, but she not to him. Al was a city dude who wore expensive loafers and shirts that had to be dry-cleaned. He marinated in expensive cologne to excess, but he was a very encouraging teacher. He told me I could be a very good if not a great accordionist. Very good is closer to the truth in retrospect.

That was the beginning of my accordion playing. The story [177] has been told other places than here. I loved the accordion and felt natural playing the instrument. I graduated very quickly from the 12-bass student model and required a full 120-bass adult model. Al suggested a

---

[176] https://en.wikipedia.org/wiki/Dick_Contino.
[177] http://www.cfa.arizona.edu/accordion/JamesO.html

Biela, a student model of the famous Petosa line, which cost $245. I did not have the money, but Dad sprang for it if we would pay him back with summer work. Mom and I picked strawberries to pay off that squeezebox and life was never the same again.

Unfortunately, the accordion craze died out within a year and there was no accordion teacher. I played at fairs, for Rotary and Lions, for church, for school and just about anywhere I was asked. Undoubtedly, in Mosier and numerous other Eastern Oregon towns, there are many homes that have one of Joe P.'s accordions in a garage, closet, basement or attic, full of mildew from being untouched after 60 years.

In addition to all this music, however, I did get a real job. Mom's connection at the packing shed in Oak Grove outside of Hood River, which was a long drive for her, resulted in a Saturday job for me. Harry H., the plant foreman, was a benevolent man. He said he could use me on Saturdays, which were short days anyway, to repair lug boxes in the attic of the packing shed. It was upstairs, dimly lit, but I was all by myself. The task was to look at the A.G.A.[178] lug box that was damaged, find another box that was damaged in a different way and cannibalize one or another to create "one" intact box. It paid something less than $1.00 per hour, but I had a time card for checking in and out, which I valued greatly. It was probably a job that was invented just for me.

More importantly, I applied and received my Social Security card at 14 years of age. Fifty years later, at age 64, I would carry that same card to the Social Security office in Tucson and apply for benefits. My relationship with A.G.A. endured for several years, even while in college. They were glad to hire seasonal workers to harvest and preserve the abundance of Bartlett, D'anjou and Bosque pears, not to mention Gravenstein, Newton and Delicious apples. Those were the robust fruits in the 1950s, long before we had Asian pears, Honey Crisp apples and many hybrids. And that Social Security number has followed me for years, whether applying for a job, having my credit checked or filing a return with the I.R.S. Thank you, FDR, for bringing that safety net to all Americans.[179]

After the departure en masse of Al D. and Joe P., I needed an accordion teacher. We found Mr. B. in The Dalles and lessons became a Saturday trip to his tiny house. He would write pseudo-Bach endings and provide non-harmonic additions to some of the simple tunes I was playing. Soon

---

[178] http://www.oregonencyclopedia.org/articles/pears_the_pear_industry/#.ViD6dsu4mMI

[179] http://www.ssa.gov/history/bane2.html

afterwards upon exploration in Hood River, we found the American Music Company, a music store on the Heights managed by Karl K., who would become not only my accordion teacher, but also a lifelong friend and mentor.

Karl was an excellent teacher who demanded correct fingering, controlled dynamics and precise performance, not merely showmanship. An excellent musician himself, which, I believe came from his time in the Navy band, he incorporated music theory in every lesson. The Stradella bass [180] used in piano-accordions, mirrors the circle of fifths inherent in Western classical music since the Common Practice period of the Eighteenth Century.[181] All those buttons for the left hand indeed meant something and your fingers had to learn, sans sight, where to move. Karl showed me how to combine buttons to create richer harmony. His tutelage certainly gave me a foot up on music theory, which I eventually studied in college as a music major.

Accordions were popular throughout the 1940s and 1950s, and then they died out. They are making a comeback now, at least according to some sources.[182] Since Dick Contino was a matinee idol of that day[183] and students wanted to play like him, this popularity created a teaching demand that Karl could not satisfy. By the time I was sixteen, he felt I was advanced enough to be a teacher. At first, I gave lessons at his studio in Hood River, charging $2.00 per lesson. He received 25% of that for studio rent. Karl and his spouse, who helped in the store, would leave at 6 p.m. I would teach lessons and manage the store in their absence, which was quite a responsibility for a junior in high school.

After I inherited my sister's 1941 Chevy, Karl established a studio for me in the Parkdale Elementary School in Hood River's upper valley. Cascade Locks was also on my beat and I traveled to students' homes and gave lessons in their parlors or kitchens. Some students were young while others were senior citizens. It was quite an experience but it seemed a natural part of my life then.

In the fall of my senior year, since I had almost enough credits to graduate, I worked at night at the A.G.A. cannery in Hood River, 4 p.m. to 1 a.m., fronting up at school for the second period but leaving after the sixth. In addition, I was still teaching lessons on Saturdays. I also made a fortnightly trip to Portland on the Greyhound to study accordion with

---

[180] https://en.wikipedia.org/wiki/Stradella_bass_system
[181] http://thegreathistoryofarts.weebly.com/common-practice-era.html
[182] http://www.theatlantic.com/entertainment/archive/2014/01/accordions-so-hot-right-now/282782/
[183] http://www.petosa.com/contino/

Luigi R.. It didn't leave much time for homework, but I was a quick study.

One morning, rather blurry eyed, I arrived at school before second period, which was Modern Problems, and was advised we were having a quiz on the President's cabinet. Who were they?[184] I looked at a list, memorized it quickly and passed the text 100%. But I don't think it shifted into long-term memory, except I know the President was Dwight D. Eisenhower, so Richard M. Nixon was probably his Vice President. In our Democratic household, I did not care for either.

I think I discovered at that point in my life that I have more energy than can be consumed with a single focus and could multi-task, long before that term entered our patois. Too, I didn't need eight hours of sleep every night. Finally, it would be hard to choose what I was going to be in life when so many pursuits fascinated me.

When the cannery season was over mid-November, I added first period bookkeeping and business law to my course of study at the high school. I had to make up what I had missed from September, but the course was a project based on an actual business. You had to take all the income and expenditures from a fictitious business, with invoices and receipts, and run the numbers for a year. I loved it and should have realized then, and not in 1984, that I was cut out to be an M.B.A. Live and learn.

In the spring of 1957, my senior year, in anticipation of possibly majoring in music in college, I began piano work with Mildred W., a teacher at Roth's Music Store in The Dalles. She was a good teacher who had an M.A. in piano performance. She introduced Czerny *Studies*, then some Chopin as well as the requisite Bach *Two-part Inventions*. This was a late age to begin piano study, but I could read adequately and had basic technique. Had I begun with her at age ten or so, I might have been a very good pianist in college rather than mediocre.

Sometime in April of that year, Ernie S., who was now the principal of Mosier High School passed me in the parking lot and said: "Do you have your speech ready for graduation?" I guess that meant that I was the Valedictorian. I made it without trying. June P. would be Salutatorian, but I would have the final word. Six senior boys and six senior girls prepared for their last month of public school. There was the super secret senior sneak, which the entire school knew about, to a dude ranch outside of La Grande, Oregon.

---

[184] http://www.infoplease.com/ipa/A0101255.html

About this time, The Dalles Dam was nearing completion and the floodgates were closed. On March 10, 1957, the reservoir behind the dam began to fill, which eliminated historic Celilo Falls,[185] a trading area for over a thousand years before. The Feds had already flooded the First Americans' fishing grounds at Kettle Falls [186] or Shonitkwu, when Grand Coulee Dam was completed in 1940. This was no great loss to Anglos, who needed the power to light up their homes and industry in the Northwest. The tribes received money, but it was inadequate to what was surrendered to "progress". I enjoy seeing the present day casinos scattered about the country and smilingly think: "Native Americans lost the battle but they certainly won the war!"

I vaguely remember March 10, but am embarrassed to say not as a profound destruction of something of such historic and cultural importance. I was more worried about my future and registering with the Selective Service.[187] Would college be part of the equation for my next step in life? There were neither senior counselors to help one apply nor college visitations. No 529 College Savings funds. No recruiters. Neither S.A.T.'s nor A.C.T.'s.[188] No essays. No interviews. No scholarships for valedictorians. How did I ever get to college? How did anyone? Surprisingly, five of my classmates plus I made it.

---

[185] http://www.historylink.org/index.cfm?DisplayPage=output.cfm&file_id=10010
[186] https://en.wikipedia.org/wiki/Kettle_Falls,_Washington
[187] https://en.wikipedia.org/wiki/Selective_Service_System
[188] https://en.wikipedia.org/wiki/College_entrance_exam

Chapter 13 Halting Steps Toward Adulthood

I did not have a summer job after I graduated from high school. Classmates scattered and I figured I could make some fast cash picking cherries. However, a chance visit with Gil and Helen G. in Ariel, Washington, provided an employment opportunity. A forest fire lookout employee on one of the stations had bailed out because his live-in girl friend had tossed his typewriter over the bluff before hiking down the trail in a fit of anger. He decided he did not want to stay either.

With the fire season upon the Gifford Pinchot Forest [189] in Washington State, a forest lookout was needed immediately at Smith Creek Lookout, six miles east of Mt. St. Helens, much higher and seemingly a dormant volcano in those years. This was Saturday and I would need to be back for the job on Monday. We rushed home, conferred with George C., a neighbor who was a ranger in that same forest, bought groceries and I was delivered back to the Ranger Station the next day. I did not even have the opportunity to decide what I was going to do after high school. It was done for me.

As it turned out, the need to staff that lookout was highly overrated and I was told I would stay in a tent at the Ranger Station, as the other employees arrived to clean trails and provide fire support. We were all sent to a fire-fighting school in Stevenson, Washington for a week with other fire-fighters from different ranger districts in the forest. Most of the guys were college men from the east coast, many majoring in forestry or civil engineering. They were very inspiring to me as they shared their knowledge and college experience. I knew college was in the future for me.

Eventually, I was transported to Smith Creek Lookout,[190] which was a six-mile hike from a logging road, by mule train. Two mules carried my supplies plus my Biela accordion, which I was encouraged to take along. The tower was 20 feet high, the top of which was a one-room structure, windows all around, from which fires were located and reported.[191] One accomplished the required duties in those cramped quarters, as well as the cooking, eating and sleeping. In those days, the lookout, the person, that is, had a circular map that could locate the azimuth of a fire. Another lookout station in the forest at some distance would report the same fire, which could then be pinpointed in a specific section through triangulation. There was a two-way radio among the fire stations for communication.

---

[189] http://www.fs.usda.gov/giffordpinchot/
[190] http://www.firetower.org/lookouts/Lookout.aspx?id=1344
[191] https://en.wikipedia.org/wiki/Fire_lookout_tower

It was a lonely job and there were few fires that summer. But other responsibilities included cleaning trails on cloudy days, carrying drinking and washing water as well as painting the lookout tower, tool shed and privy. I kept busy but was glad when I left in September, with lots of money in the bank for college.

Rather than beginning college that fall, I delayed to earn additional money at the A.G.A. plant in Hood River, pushing and pulling fruit boxes. I quickly reaffirmed this was not what I was going to be doing the rest of my life. On October 4, 1957 we entered the space age, when the U.S.S.R. launched an unmanned satellite into orbit around the earth, Sputnik.[192] That was scary, knowing how precarious and volatile our relationship was with Russia. It certainly pushed the United States out of space complacency and led to our being first on the moon 12 years later.[193] And it also made American educators rethink the curricula to include more science and math. I don't think Mosier High School obtained another microscope, however.

I found space travel, just to the moon, a fascinating possibility after seeing the 1950 movie, *Destination Moon*.[194] Even now, I went to see *The Martian*[195] the day it arrived in the theaters in October 2015, finding it difficult to believe that will not be a possibility during my lifetime, but sometime in the 2030s. May it be so but unlike the movie or Andy Weir's incredible book.[196] I have pondered why we have so dropped the ball on space travel yet can spend such excess on wars in Iraq[197] and Afghanistan.[198]

I made a few trips to Portland State College that autumn to get set up for classes. I liked Portland and had taken accordion lessons there. My sister attended for a term or two and my brother completed his first two years of an engineering degree before transferring to Oregon State College at Corvallis. I felt comfortable in Portland. Furthermore, I wanted an urban college, not one with campus traditions and all the rah-rah that freshmen endure on a resident campus.

---

[192] http://www.history.com/this-day-in-history/sputnik-launched
[193] http://www.nasa.gov/mission_pages/apollo/apollo11.html
[194] https://en.wikipedia.org/wiki/Destination_Moon_(film)
[195] http://www.imdb.com/title/tt3659388/
[196] http://andyweirauthor.com/books/the-martian-hc
[197] http://www.reuters.com/article/2013/03/14/us-iraq-war-anniversary-idUSBRE92D0PG20130314
[198] http://time.com/3651697/afghanistan-war-cost/

Tuition was only $45 a term but books would probably add another $20-$30 to my college expenses. I rented an apartment four blocks from campus with a Murphy bed and was all ready in January 1958. I took a full load, world history, music theory, English, physical education, introduction to education and a few other subjects and paid for it all from my savings account. I figured I would attend until I ran out of money, find another job and save, return to college until I graduated. As it turned out, I graduated in three and a half years and held a tuition scholarship for every term except my first. Dad wanted me to keep attending and funded me fully after that first year.

Many of those starting college in January were in the same classes as I, with the exception of music theory. There were many veterans who had served in Korea who were in their mid-twenties. They immediately became my circle of friends. Dick S. and Ken G. were special friends. We were all new to college, most of us first generation, and were running a little scared. Some of them had spouses and even children. We would gather together to study at various locations.

On my nineteenth birthday, several friends gathered at my apartment. I was not old enough to buy beer, but my buddies were. A few six-packs for them and a couple of stubbies for me and I was drunk. I had never been before and it was a rather nice feeling, not drunk on my butt, but just tipsy. These guys pulled down the Murphy bed that night and tucked me in before they left. No way was I to leave the apartment after drinking with my friends.

On Fridays, after class, my older friends would gather at a local pub for a few rounds of beer to top off the week, even possibly a successful test. The strategy for us was to find a booth and I'd disappear to the restroom. The bartender would bring a pitcher of beer, I'd return to the booth and I was never asked for my I.D. Things were loose around Portland State in those days and it was great fun. When I finally turned 21 in March 1960, it was no longer necessary to play this tavern game. But I was proud to vote in the presidential election that November,[199] casting my ballot for JFK, who seemed to represent the next generation of which I was a member.

My musical studies were excellent. I jumped into the second term of music theory without the first, floundered for a few weeks until I figured out what John S. meant by parallel fifths and direct octaves, and then did pretty well. My first European history test with Dr. Basil D., who was a clotheshorse par excellence and a gifted linguist, fluent in six languages, was tenuous. I was certain I had flunked. How elated I was

---

[199] http://www.ushistory.org/us/56a.asp

when I found I had earned an A-, but several of my buddies, not acclimated to an academic setting and lacking writing skills, indeed did flunk. I became the "go-to-guy" after that. Everyone wanted to study with me and I enjoyed sharing my knowledge and study skills.

My piano teacher, Sylvia K. had a studio in the Fine Arts Building across from the Olds and King department store.[200] I had a half hour lesson once a week playing her recently purchased nine-foot Steinway grand piano. Walking in the pouring Portland rain to get to my lesson and classes was common. Miss K. found my phrasing "odd" but coached me faithfully for three and a half years, until I could produce a fair rendition of Beethoven's *First Piano Concerto in C, opus 15* [201] with the school orchestra my senior year.

I was never a concert pianist. I learned pieces and had reasonably good technique but never felt comfortable seated in front of that big machine with white and black keys, reciting a memorized piece by myself, while the world listened. I began formal piano study too late in life. However, I did become a pretty competent accompanist, preferring second-fiddle position to that of concertmaster. It was not until I was about 50 that I came back to the accordion, my instrument of choice. I had abandoned it at Portland State when the head of the music department, John S., queried: "You play what?" Only in Europe's conservatories or select California or Canadian colleges could one major in accordion.

College was a world of discoveries. I could not be content with a full load of 15 units, but crowded my schedule with things I did not need to graduate, including cultural anthropology, industrial psychology [202] and even French. I resented I had to declare "one" major, which was music education. I would become a music teacher. It's what everyone expected I would do and I did not disappoint anyone. I graduated in June 1961 *magna cum laude* [203] and got to walk across the stage first with four others who had managed to achieve a high grade point average before the masses were awarded their diplomas. I was first-generation college but second in the family, since brother Tom had graduated Oregon State College the year before, the same year my future spouse had graduated. But I didn't know this until years later.

Now what? The train, or as it became, a jet plane, went somewhere. It was the Lone Star state.

---

[200] https://www.cardcow.com/325180/olds-wortman-king-department-store-portland-oregon/
[201] http://imslp.org/wiki/Piano_Concerto_No.1,_Op.15_(Beethoven,_Ludwig_van)
[202] present usage is Organization Psychology
[203] http://www.investopedia.com/terms/m/magna-cum-laude.asp

Chapter 14   Nervous Over Military Service

It was the middle of June 1961 and my college days were over. Dad pulled my 22-foot house trailer, in which I had lived in Parkrose, back to Mosier. In the Spring Term of my senior year, I had been a student teacher in Parkrose and even accompanied the high school production of *South Pacific* that spring. I was committed to join the Oregon Air National Guard as part of my national service, but had neither taken the oath nor signed the papers.

As a graduation celebration, I hopped on a Greyhound bus and went to Long Beach, California, to visit Tom, Glada and their two daughters, Colleen and Kris. It was a fun two weeks. I visited the Marine recruiting station and almost joined the Marine Reserves, thinking I would be stationed at Camp Pendleton. The tour of duty was six months, plus five and a half years of reserve, unless you were called up for active duty. Although I really loved the warmth of Southern California, I deferred and returned to Mosier. I signed the papers in Portland to join the Air Guard. The plane, not a train, went somewhere and that somewhere was Lackland Air Force Base [204] in San Antonio, Texas around the middle of July. It was my first plane trip and the craft was a DC-8.

What a change for a pampered college guy. The ANG (Air National Guard) group, called a flight, was all college grads, many with advanced degrees, including LLDs. The weather was tremendously oppressive in July, humidity almost the same as the temperature, high 80s or low 90s. I was shocked and overwhelmed with the military, but managed to survive basic training for eight weeks without a court martial.

It was particularly alarming to all on August 13, 1961, when we heard the German Democratic Republic (East Germany) had walled off the Russian sector from the West.[205] Our drill instructor taunted us with the notion we had better pack our duffle bags because we were shipping out to Berlin's Tempelhof Airport. It never happened for my flight, however. And that wall stood for three decades until Reagan [206] managed to hector Gorbachev into dismantling it in the early 1990s. What history. In 1980, on a guided tour, I remember passing through Checkpoint Charlie [207] and observing the bleakness of the Communist side. It's all one Germany now.

---

[204] https://en.wikipedia.org/wiki/Lackland_Air_Force_Base
[205] https://en.wikipedia.org/wiki/Berlin_Wall
[206] http://www.historyplace.com/speeches/reagan-tear-down.htm
[207] https://www.berlin.de/orte/sehenswuerdigkeiten/checkpoint-charlie/index.en.php

At the conclusion of basic training, I was shipped to Lowry Air Force Base,[208] in Denver, Colorado, for another three months to attend munitions school. I was a bomb roller and learned how to deal with 50 mm ammo, carbines, grenades, poison gas, napalm and hydrogen bombs. I also worked on ordnance disposal on a bombing range outside of Aurora, Colorado. It was not a first love for me, but I had great companions, all regular Air Force personnel, who bonded with me as we went through the school. I also discovered Boulder and the University of Colorado and thought that would be a great place for a graduate degree in music. What do munitions and music have in common? They both begin with "mu".

My brother had served his country and it seemed I could do no less. But I did live under the apprehension that my unit could be mobilized at any time, war or peace, when the need arose from floods, fires, natural disasters or even the Vietnam War. It never happened and I served six months active duty and five and a half years in the reserves, rising to the rank of E-5 (staff sergeant) through weekend drills once a month plus two weeks of annual summer camp. My unit was part of the ADC (Air Defense Command),[209] which meant homeland security, particularly of the skies over the fifty states.

Some men are born soldiers; others tolerate it because of national need. I was definitely in the latter category. But I enjoyed fellow airmen at Lowry as well as Portland Airport, where we had weekend drills and summer camp. Serving in the military gives one a broadened perspective on life as well as camaraderie with others who have been in the service. You understand the enlisted personnel versus officers' dichotomy as well as the hierarchy of rank, not to mention surviving basic training. And there are some things you understand because you have been in the locker room together, which can't be explained to those without military experience.

It was now the middle of December when I arrived back in Mosier without a job or any specific future plans. Within a few days, Ernie S., who was still principal at Mosier School, knocked on our door and asked if I would substitute for a few months. The math teacher, Brad B., had contracted hepatitis and would probably be out for the rest of the school year. Would I like to substitute for him?

But the assignment was math, which included General Math and Algebra I, which would be no problem for me. There was also Algebra II and geometry, which would be a greater challenge. He brought the books

---

[208] http://www.lowrydenver.com/art-and-history/
[209] http://www.afhra.af.mil/factsheets/factsheet.asp?id=10954

the next day and said I would need to be ready the first school day of the New Year, 1962. Fortunately, he brought the answer books and I managed to stay one page ahead of the kids.

Jesus was not readily accepted in his home community. "Is this the carpenter's son", they queried? [210] I thought I would find a similar circumstance. It is probably not wise to return to your hometown, whether Mosier or Nazareth. And my general plan had been to seek a job in Portland or Los Angeles. It was a quirky turn of events. But, surprisingly, I was well accepted and respected in my community. The students had not advanced in math, regardless where they were in their texts. I had to do a great deal of remedial work in all classes. This bought me time to master the content myself.

I demanded homework, corrected it and pointed out mistakes. I presented real lessons motivating the students to attend and absorb what I was discussing, using a variety of aids, and then demonstrating the mathematical principle and why it was important. I finally assigned work to reinforce the concept and master the mathematical calculation. Although I was learning with the students, the problem with this type of "seat of the pants" teaching is you do not always understand why you do something. Deep knowledge of a subject allows one to deal with the "why" questions.

Community feedback was very good and I was offered a job for the following year, teaching math and music K-12 in this one-building school. Ernie S. said I would need to become certified with a math minor. Thank goodness for correspondence courses. Consolidation of Mosier High School was planned with a school district in The Dalles after this one year. One more year in the small town meant I would be first in line for a credible job in the new district in The Dalles. Surprisingly, the salary was as good as I would have received in a much larger school district in California. Mom and Dad were willing for me to live at home. I agreed to pay room and board to assist with food and utilities. The little cabin off from the house became my area for sleeping and grading papers.

---

[210] http://biblehub.com/mark/6-4.htm

Chapter 15   Music Maestro and Math Mentor

Do teachers nowadays negotiate their class-load and assignment? We certainly did not in 1962. My first teaching position at Mosier was seven periods, which included band, general music for the K-6 grades, general math, Algebra I and college prep math for a small group of college-bound seniors. Of my forty-two years in the classroom, this year was one of my most rewarding. I loved it. Teachers were respected in Mosier and I was a teacher. Mosier was a one-building school, with five elementary and eight high school teachers. I knew most of the teachers, having been a student there, but I was never treated like a neophyte. This was a professional job and I was treated as a professional.

The band was abysmal, a combination of every sort of instrument one could imagine, with skill levels from "which end do I blow in?" to "which pitches are flatted in the key of D-flat?" These country kids wanted to make music, so by rote, note and determination, we performed at the Christmas program.

The math teaching was rewarding as well. I had taken math courses toward my required certification the prior summer and had a better understanding of what I was doing. Teaching trigonometry was a real challenge, however, but I had mastered some of the mysteries of the right triangle. As a result, we measured the school flagpole and the height of the school building without climbing to the top. There were few discipline problems in or out of class.

I had good relationships with the other teachers. A few of the normal-school women who taught in the elementary grades asked to observe my teaching. They were working on their B.S., now required for certification, and needed to observe other classrooms. That was the ultimate compliment, because they had been teachers there when I was merely in the seventh grade. A particular friend was Jim C., fourth grade teacher, from Louisiana. He took teaching seriously, but not so seriously that we couldn't down a few beers after class on Friday. For him, however, it was usually Scotch, which I never could tolerate.

We brought great humor, spirit and gossip to the faculty room, where it seemed everyone was a Marlboro man or Winston woman. If one did not smoke, they certainly were subject to secondary smoke. Little did we know in those days of the Surgeon General's warning that would come in 1964. [211] We must have reeked of nicotine when we returned to our classrooms. I would continue to smoke until I was almost 30 years old

---

[211] http://www.health.harvard.edu/blog/surgeon-generals-1964-report-making-smoking-history-201401106970

and finally got the message. I had picked up the habit from older siblings, who supplied my addiction. However, when I tried to buy cigarettes from Mr. A.'s market in Mosier in the eighth grade, he sold them to me but reported to Dad.

Mosier teachers were committed to small schools and country kids, but we had no compunction about discussing students in the faculty break room. The 1962-63 school year would be Mosier High School's last, since the district was consolidated by election with Chenowith District #9 in The Dalles. A new high school would be formed.

Although a new building was not completed for two more years, the new school was called Wahtonka High [212] and the mascot was an eagle. School consolidation was rampant in the 1960s, particularly to pool resources, save tax dollars and provide students with a more varied course of study,[213] particularly in the aftermath of Sputnik. Science was critical and "new-math" the order of the day. Like all change, there was the good, bad and the ugly. The value system of students from the Chenowith area was different from Mosier students. Many providers worked at the Harvey Aluminum plant. [214] This smelter came into the area in 1958 and closed in 2000, due to bankruptcy.[215] The social dynamic of Wahtonka was different because of the transient nature of plant work, which employed many providers in the area. Discipline issues were more prevalent.

I was teaching third-period band when Ernie S., principal, announced on the perennially invasive intercom that President Kennedy had been shot and wounded in Dallas.[216] It was Friday, November 22, 1963, shortly before noon in our time zone. The announcement quickly followed that he was dead. This was a blow to the school and nothing could be accomplished the remainder of the day. School was dismissed early. I was devastated since I had voted for JFK, my first opportunity to participate in a national election. He was now gone and Lyndon B. Johnson became the 36th President of the United States.[217] The vision of JFK had been replaced by old school politics. Little did we know, then,

---

[212] https://www.facebook.com/WahtonkaHighSchool
[213] http://www.ericdigests.org/pre-925/school.htm
[214] http://blogs.dailybreeze.com/history/2015/04/18/harvey-aluminum-in-harbor-gateways-long-sometimes-turbulent-history/
[215] http://www.flatheadnewsgroup.com/hungryhorsenews/seven-regional-aluminum-plants-gone/article_9ef13c54-d3dd-11e0-9d88-001cc4c002e0.html
[216] http://www.jfklibrary.org/JFK/JFK-in-History/November-22-1963-Death-of-the-President.aspx
[217] https://en.wikipedia.org/wiki/Lyndon_B._Johnson

what LBJ would do to provide medical insurance for the aged and Civil Rights for minorities.

There was no school the following week, which would have been Monday through Wednesday only, since it was Thanksgiving week. Mom and I stayed glued to the television to watch the funeral,[218] a sad time for America. Four times in our history a President has been assassinated: Lincoln in 1865, Garfield in 1881 and McKinley in 1901.[219] Never before, though, had the tragedy been played out so immediately on black and white television. For my generation, it was our day of infamy as much as Pearl Harbor had been for earlier citizens or 9-11 for millennials.

During this period, I began working on a master's degree at Central Washington College in Ellensburg.[220] Few teachers in the district had a master's degree. I had begun graduate study at Portland State the prior summer, but felt I would have the same professors as I had had in undergraduate school. I wanted new ways of thinking, not just more research papers. Central was a good fit for me. I stayed in a dorm for the summer and had different roommates and new professors. I picked up courses that would enhance my professional resume as well as provide new teaching strategies. Like many regional colleges in those days, Central was basically an old normal school that had transitioned into a four-year institution. Within a few years, colleges like this would transition once again into universities, offering even more varied curricula and more advanced degrees.

I skipped school the summer of 1964 and took a road trip for sheer adventure. It was not exactly Route 66[221] but I was on that famous road for part of the trip. I drove to Montana, then Utah, Arizona and California, ending up for a visit with my brother and family in Long Beach, California. I could not be gone for more than a month because I had Air Guard duties one weekend each month. It was a liberating experience to see "Big Sky" country as well as the great Southwest. I knew I could live other places than Oregon.

My big purchase in 1965 was a slightly used Steinway[222] grand piano, M model, for $3000. Although it has been moved eight times since then, I still have it and enjoy playing it. I wanted to be a better pianist and

---

[218] http://www.jfklibrary.org/JFK/JFK-in-History/November-22-1963-Death-of-the-President.aspx?p=3
[219] http://www.presidentsusa.net/assassinations.html
[220] https://en.wikipedia.org/wiki/Central_Washington_University
[221] http://www.historic66.com
[222] http://www.steinway.com/about/history/

thought this would help. Imagine my parent's surprise when Jim S.'s delivery truck from Salem pulled into the Mosier driveway and moved a 5'10" mahogany grand into the living room. Dad immediately ran to the basement to reinforce the floor joist. It must have weighed a ton and he could see it falling through the floor into the mucky basement below. It never happened though. I used this instrument to practice and prepare my Master's recital, which I presented the summer of 1966 on a nine-foot Bösendorfer piano [223] in the Hertz recital hall on Central's campus. I had completed my master's degree.

My four years of teaching in District #9 turned a little stale. Some years, I was the itinerant music specialist in the elementary schools, others, I was entirely in the high school, teaching basic math and band. There were good friends and lots of Friday afternoon gatherings at Ole's Supper Club,[224] a local watering hole in The Dalles, to critique our week in the classroom and solve all the problems of education. I had dates with teachers but nothing serious ever developed. We were seeking fun and relief from teaching with others who had the same job. I wanted more and began to explore options. Should I go to graduate school to earn a Ph.D. or would I find a teaching job somewhere else? As it turned out, I had my choice between the two.

I searched for teaching opportunities in Hawaii, where I had never been. I interviewed with a recruiter in Portland and was offered a contract at Hickam Air Force Base, [225] near Honolulu on Oahu. But the feelers I had sent out to major universities about a Ph.D. in music transpired as well. I was awarded a one-year fellowship at the University of Colorado [226] at Boulder, with a stipend that matched my current teaching salary after taxes. It was a no-brainer. I would be off to Boulder [227] in the fall, having finished my master's recital and thesis at Central Washington. I could go to Hawaii after graduate school.

It was the autumn of 1966. I headed east on I-84, not on a train but in a packed 1962 Corvair Monza, [228] to Boulder, my home for the next two years. I would be returning to a region where I had been stationed in the Air Force and whose seasons I enjoyed, particularly skiing in dry powder.

---

[223] https://en.wikipedia.org/wiki/Bösendorfer
[224] https://www.etsy.com/listing/75543644/oles-supper-club-old-neon-sign-red-white
[225] http://www.military.com/base-guide/hickam-air-force-base
[226] https://en.wikipedia.org/wiki/University_of_Colorado
[227] https://en.wikipedia.org/wiki/Boulder,_Colorado
[228] http://auto.howstuffworks.com/1962-1964-chevrolet-corvair-monza-spyder.htm

Chapter 16   Ph.D. = Piled Higher and Deeper

The two years I spent in Boulder at the University of Colorado were some of the most formative experiences I have ever had. I became me. I lived at Williams Village, a new high-rise twin tower for graduate students about a mile from campus. I choose to room alone because I wanted to devote my time to study, exclusively. The largesse of a University Fellowship provided $250 a month for me, which was slightly less than I was clearing a month as a public school teacher in The Dalles. I had savings as well.

The entrance exams were not difficult, just vague questions about pedagogical principles and designing a unit of instruction in music. This was followed by interviews with my major professors. There were three in my area, Bill R., my doctoral adviser, a sweetheart of a professor, Gordon S. and Sally M. They were well-known Ph.Ds. in their field and I was honored to study with them. There was a variety of courses for the Ph.D. It took two years to complete the course work and a year for the dissertation, for which I was advised to plan early in the course of study.

Colorado is a beautiful area, particularly Boulder, which sits on the front range of the Rockies. The flatirons [229] define the area, beautiful sandstone rocks against a pine forest. The weather can be severe and that is probably why NCAR (National Center for Atmospheric Research) [230] is located in Boulder. Although I had trepidation whether I was doctoral material and could finish this degree, I loved living in Boulder. The weather would be sunny and warm one day, snowy the next.

In those days, the Ph.D. required reading comprehension in two languages. For me, it was French, which I knew a little, and German, which I knew not at all. I enrolled in a German cram course to pass the exam in language comprehension. We were required to read German in Gothic script, [231] which might be useful in research for a dissertation. Two other students, both doctoral applicants, were enrolled with me, Ron W. and Richard S., who would become bosom buddies for the rest of our lives. We were all running scared because of what the Ph.D. required, but managed to work in some social time together. Ron W. invited me to his house for Thanksgiving the first year, and I became part of that family. Both Ron and Richard would eventually follow me back to Oregon to teach at the same college at which I was a faculty member.

---

[229] https://en.wikipedia.org/wiki/Flatirons
[230] https://ncar.ucar.edu/about-ncar
[231] https://script.byu.edu/SiteAssets/overview.pdf

Ron had a booming *basso profundo* voice and sang several opera roles in his career. Marilyn, his spouse, was a classroom teacher and music specialist. There were five children, two boys and three girls. By contrast, Richard S. was single and had just finished a piano masters at the Eastman School of Music. [232] It is strange how a "trapped in an elevator" scenario produces lifelong friends. We began the German class with thirty doctoral students from various disciplines across campus but ended the semester four months later with just the three of us plus the old German master. We prevailed and all passed the German language exam a few weeks later.

My love of skiing, which I had learned in the mountains of Oregon, where the snow is always wet, was greatly enhanced in the dry powder of Colorado. Eldora Mountain Resort [233] was barely 30 miles from the campus, and Winterpark, [234] a weekend trip, had dream runs. Many classes at The University of Colorado were not held on Friday, which gave students (and we suspected, professors) a three-day weekend to ski, if not study. The standing joke among the faculty at the University of Colorado was: "The pay is not good, but you have the Rockies."

The essence of any Ph.D. is not the courses you take, but, rather, comprehensive exams that qualify one as a scholar in his or her field. I began preparing for those comprehensive exams the minute I was in the program. It took two years to complete the required work, which included courses in educational psychology, music theory, history and education. I took additional courses in counterpoint and history of music notation, which could be done on an audit basis.

Through all of this, I was a member of the Oregon Air National Guard and took my monthly training at Aurora, where the Colorado Air Guard was based. We rolled bombs, painted 50 mm ammo and listened to the first Super Bowl on radio on January 15, 1967 between the Green Bay Packers and Kansas City Chiefs. [235] The Colorado Guard kept its weekend warriors busier than in Oregon. There were always projects to complete on the duty weekend, grunt work that the regulars did not want to do.

I experienced dorm life and college rah-rah at Colorado. My second year, I was a resident adviser in Williams Village, supervising two floors of undergraduates. I also ran the social program for the entire Village. There was plenty of money to throw parties and I did. The "woodsy" was

---

[232] http://www.esm.rochester.edu
[233] http://www.visitingboulder.com/skiing-near-boulder.php
[234] http://www.colorado.com/cities-and-towns/winter-park
[235] https://en.wikipedia.org/wiki/Super_Bowl_I

a favorite, basically a kegger held in a forest location. Favorite haunts on the "hill" above the University were the Sink and Tulagi's, both of which served 3.2 beer to 18- year olds. I would buy out the club for an evening for Village residents and have an open bar.

I had lots of friends in those days, running with a group of fellow students, sometimes with a date but often without. It really filled in a phase of my college development, which I never experienced in the urban setting of Portland State College. I feel my experience at Colorado was the "true" college experience, living, studying and partying with other students, many of who were years younger than I.

Sally M. asked me to teach a music education class at the Denver Center, which was an extension of the University. I drove the twenty miles weekly to the city campus and felt I was finally a college professor. I enjoyed the urban nature of big town Denver but did not aspire to city life for the future. I decided to look for a position in a small college in the Western states.

In the summer of my second year at Boulder, I took my comprehensive exams followed by the orals and was admitted to candidacy. At this time, my dissertation proposal to conduct a control-experimental study on the efficacy of shape notes [236] with fifth graders was accepted. I choose to use the seven-note system, which was similar to George Kyme's classic study.[237] Doctoral research purported to foster new research, but it was acceptable to replicate an earlier study. All I needed was two classes of fifth graders to begin the study. That happened during my spring break of 1968, when I returned to Oregon for a week.

Although the University did not provide a fellowship for my second year of study, I was paid to be a resident advisor at Williams Village at the University. The university musicologist needed a reader for his correspondence class, which paid $1.00 per assignment submitted. There was a backlog of over 300 papers, so I took that job as well. The monthly National Guard training contributed to my bank account and I still had savings. I thought I would remain for a third year at Boulder and re-applied for a fellowship, which I was awarded. I had to reject it, however, for a fortuitous reason: I had a professorship at an Oregon college.

During the spring of my second year at Boulder, I sent out letters of inquiry to colleges, in both Oregon and Washington. There was an

---

[236] https://en.wikipedia.org/wiki/Shape_note
[237] http://www.jstor.org/stable/3344231?seq=1#page_scan_tab_contents

elementary music methods position at Eastern Oregon College [238] at La Grande that was particularly attractive, but it was filled internally. The only positive response I received was from Ed S., head of the music department at Oregon College of Education in Monmouth. Would I come for an interview? You bet.

During my Spring Break, Mom and Dad picked me up at the Portland International Airport and we drove to Monmouth. Ed interviewed me with some senior faculty members and outlined the position, which was a split assignment with the Campus Elementary School, half as music specialist there and half teaching music education courses to majors in the college. He asked me to return later that week for another series of interviews, which included the Dean of Faculty, Bert K., the Department Chair of Education, Don D. as well as the President, Leonard R. There was no indication I had the job, but the Saturday before I was to fly back to Colorado, Ed and his spouse Evelyn happened to be traveling on I-84. He found where we lived in Mosier, stopped by the house and said I had the job, if I wanted it. I did.

---

[238] https://www.eou.edu

Chapter 17   Dream Job, For A While

Although I still had to complete my comprehensive and oral exams, I returned to the University of Colorado amid congratulations that I actually had a job for the next year. In addition, I was attached to an elementary school where I would have subjects for the research required in my dissertation.

To celebrate the new position, I sold my beloved Corvair and ordered a 1968 Mercury Cougar.[239] It was a beautiful car, small V-8, with some options. It looked like a diminutive Lincoln Continental with sequential lights as turn indicators. I drove it back from Colorado loaded with my clothes, books and Head skis attached to a roof rack. There was an unfurnished apartment near Oregon College, which would become my home. The Steinway was moved from Mosier and I just needed only to buy some furniture. The local furniture store in Monmouth extended credit and I soon had a decent bed, dining table and a black Naugahyde [240] sofa, which I came to hate, plus assorted lamps and rugs. It was an old apartment, but close enough to walk to work, which was convenient in good weather but tedious in the winter rains of Western Oregon.

Half of my assignment started after Labor Day, when the elementary school began. The school was K-6, two rooms for each grade. I was to present music to each class plus teach beginning band. It was an overload assignment for a half-time position. Another surprise was that the principal, Dale H. organized outdoor-school at Silver Creek Falls [241] for bonding purposes. It was a different experience, teachers living in cabins with their students. I had the job of campfire sing-a-longs. It seemed like a long three days, but we hiked, ate and enjoyed camp life. Later in the month, college classes commenced and I picked up two music fundamentals classes as the other half of my assignment. In addition, I began my doctoral dissertation. There was no time for social life, no time for dates, no time to party.

The music faculty was small but there was awesome talent among them. Two had performed in professional opera, another was a concert pianist and one a church organist at the First Presbyterian Church in Salem. The faculty stayed in touch with one another through weekly meetings, where policy and practice were reminded and reinforced. No one was an "artiste". Ed S. prohibited any student who was reciting to add, "He or

---

[239] http://www.cargurus.com/Cars/1968-Mercury-Cougar-Pictures-c8675
[240] https://en.wikipedia.org/wiki/Naugahyde
[241] http://www.oregonstateparks.org/index.cfm?do=parkPage.dsp_parkPage&parkId=151

she is a student of Ms. X or Dr. Y" to their program notes. He believed each was a student of the entire department, not a solo studio. This is in distinction to many music schools and conservatories where the recitalist's credentials include with whom she or he is studying as the end-all-be-all of tutelage.

On top of my many duties, as newbie in the department, I was assigned the task of managing the regional contest for high school soloists in our district. Music students at the various schools in the district, which included Salem and Eugene, would come to Oregon College and perform for judges, usually professors and professional musicians from Portland, for ratings. It was a huge job of scheduling, locating rooms, getting pianos tuned, escorting judges, gathering ratings sheets, tabulating and distributing results and paying the adjudicators at the end of the day. Administrative secretary, Pat L. was incredibly helpful in coaching me through this logistical nightmare.

The first year was so successful, I was asked (commanded?) to do it the second year. When feedback is good, success usually mandates a repeat performance. "But you're the only one who can do is so well!" The prof who had mismanaged it the prior year had been relieved when I was hired. This is typical of the way we delegate and reward success. Do it well and you will be rewarded with a repeat performance. Mess up, and you will be relieved. I was never one to mess up, at least intentionally, and I believe most people want to do well. I doubt anyone ever says to him- or herself: "I think I'll foul this up so I can be relieved of the responsibility."

In this same vein, in elementary school, I was one who finished my homework early. Thank goodness my reward was never more homework, but, rather, the opportunity to explore new interests and horizons. As was stated in a film: "Sometimes more is just more." [242]

I carved out precious time to work on my dissertation faithfully that first year. I had completed the review of literature before leaving Colorado, so I set up two groups, one experimental, one control, and then matched the groups to run the study. Groups were deemed equal by calculating their mean ages and mean IQ, as measured by the Otis Quick Test.[243] Helen A., a seasoned teacher made certain my schedule for research was optimized. I had to transcribe the set pieces of music to the seven-shape notational system by hand (no computers in those days), test each child on sight singing ability both pre- and post-test.

---

[242] https://en.wikipedia.org/wiki/Sabrina_(1995_film)
[243] http://rogercrump.pbworks.com/w/file/fetch/48878238/otis1.pdf

It was not an easy study and the statistical results demonstrated no difference existed between the two groups. In short, one could learn to read music either way just as effectively. Since those days, I chuckle at teachers who claim superiority for this or that method. In short, what my study demonstrated, as similar studies have shown, if you are consistent in pedagogy, the students will learn. It probably has less to do with the system than with the consistency. And we all know many of us learn in spite of a system, a teacher or a school. We are curious human beings and will figure it out. Thank goodness brain development does not depend wholly on systems, schools or parents.

In February 1969, I met my future wife, Shirley K., who was a curriculum consultant for the Marion County Intermediate Educational School District.[244] She brought a Zuckerman harpsichord [245] to a voice class at Oregon College, where I was accompanying students on Italian arias. I had never played a harpsichord before and I had never met such a lovely lady before, classy, quick and beautiful. It wasn't love at first sight for either. She was wary of romance and I was still working on my dissertation. But romance is never far from a healthy guy's *id*, so I eventually called and asked for a date.

It was dinner with prime rib, baked potatoes and Manhattans, a drink I had just discovered. Shirley had not discovered any drinks. Born and raised in the Mennonite [246] culture and faith, she had never had a drink before. It was too strong for her and she said something like: "Let me know if I end of dancing on the table". No dancing or movies in youth, but other than that, we found we had similar values and background. But it would be a long courtship, from 1969 to 1972, when we wed. She wanted to finish her doctorate. I guess she figured if I could earn a doctorate, they must be available for everyone.

The summer of 1969, I had to return to Boulder to defend my dissertation. I buried myself in a single room at Williams Village and wrote, re-wrote and re-wrote. It was a never-ending exercise with my major professor, but we eventually shaped it into a defensible document. My committee consisted of four music and one educational psychology professors. I had planned to show a video of my classroom in which I had used the shape-notes. The audio broke down and it threw off my presentation. I thought I did not do well, but I did well enough to pass. Bill. R. said he'd never seen me at a loss of words, but I was that day. That could have been the only day in my life that occurred.

---

[244] https://en.wikipedia.org/wiki/Intermediate_school_district
[245] http://www.zhi.net
[246] http://mennoniteusa.org/who-we-are/

Then the document had to be put into final shape for the library and microfiche. Before word processing software, a professional typist did all these iterations. It cost a fortune but I eventually had a document to submit to the Graduate College. After 20 years of formal education, I was now officially a Ph.D. But as it turned out, it was not to be my final degree.

Dr. Ed. S. insisted on calling me "Dr." as soon as I returned from Boulder that summer, even though the degree was not to be granted until December. But that was okay with me. He wanted his staff to have completed doctorates and I had done that.

Oregon College of Education was a good place to begin college teaching, but it was a small college with little opportunity to expand one's professional repertoire. It was small enough to know everyone in the Faculty Senate, where I served. It was difficult to do anything, professionally and personally, without everyone knowing it. I did begin writing journal articles and had several published in the *Music Educators Journal*, [247] the premier publication of music teachers nationally. There were great conferences to attend and in-service workshops to conduct for local teachers. I could have begun and ended my career there, had I chosen, but it was too comfortable. Too much same-old-same-old after five years.

I was involved with lots of accompanying, especially lyric soprano Myra B., who was completing a vocal recital at the University of Oregon. I performed J.S. Bach's *Fifth Brandenburg Concerto* [248] on the Sabathil harpsichord [249] the department had purchased. I also accompanied many student recitals just to keep my skills current. Solo work was never my forte but I loved being the background for a good vocalist or instrumentalist.

Because of the varied curriculum I had put in place, many undergraduates wanted to student teach with me at the Campus Elementary School. I had excellent students to lead into the profession, many from whom I ended up learning. The rain in Monmouth was incessant, but livable. It snowed so hard one winter that the campus was actually closed for a few days. There were job opportunities on the East coast that I toyed with, but never really sought a different position with any conviction.

---

[247] https://us.sagepub.com/en-us/nam/music-educators-journal/journal201900
[248] http://www.classicalnotes.net/classics2/brandenburg.html
[249] http://www.thecanadianencyclopedia.ca/en/article/s-sabathil-son-ltd-emc/

Shirley and I married in August 1972 and honeymooned in Europe. We flew by charter to Iceland and then Heathrow, where we had a few days in London. We visited the British Museum [250] and Tower of London.[251] This was my first taste of Europe and it was bewildering to me, using different currencies. In London, Shirley had arranged a room at the famous London Music Club, a hostel for starving music students. There was a huge grand piano in each room. The point of a honeymoon, however, is not to practice Chopin *Etudes* and Debussy *Arabesques,* so other residents generally used the big Bechstein when we were out touring. The underground was a delight in getting us around London. From there, we took a special plane to Paris, where we had a furnished room on the *Rive Gauche.* I knew enough French to confuse any issue we encountered, but it was fun. The food was incredible and prices very good, compared to nowadays.

In Paris, we found it odd that couples picked up the key to the shower, which was a communal one off the hallway, and washed together. Shirley and I, in newly wed modesty, showered separately. When we checked out of that pension, we understood why the French showered together. We thought it had to do with romance, but not really. Each time you picked up the key, there was a charge. Thus, two people in one shower made lots of sense, at least to romantic French couples.

We rented a Fiat in Paris and drove east to Germany, spending many days wandering the banks of the Mosel. The wine was delicious, the food hearty and the Zimmerfreis [252] always a surprise. I would not recommend a European honeymoon for a newly married couple, until they live with each other a while and can manage the other's sights, smells and showering habits. But we managed and we certainly became a couple very quickly as a result. When you marry at age thirty-two, you have habits from solo living that are hard to change. That soon passed however.

We attended an Oktoberfest near Munich, just about the time of the 1972 Olympics.[253] Horrific acts of terror were committed against the Israeli athletes and I believe the term "terrorist" came into everyone's vocabulary as a result. From Germany, we drove through Switzerland and part of Italy, landing for the last part of the excursion at Nice, France. The French Riviera is everything they say it is, but in those

---

[250] http://www.britishmuseum.org
[251] http://www.hrp.org.uk/TowerOfLondon/
[252] http://www.tripadvisor.com/ShowTopic-g187299-i1624-k746322-How_much_are_the_Zimmer_Frei_s_these_days-Berchtesgaden_Upper_Bavaria_Bavaria.html
[253] http://time.com/24489/munich-massacre-1972-olympics-photos/

days it was still a bargain. Here we could relax and enjoy the rest of the honeymoon. The food was delicious, especially the *prix fixe* that most restaurants offered for evening meals. The breakfasts, usually croissant and chocolate, were delivered in the room. Usually the server would enter before we were even out of bed or dressed.

It was a wonderful honeymoon that lasted a month. There were so many events we just fell upon in Europe, from sleeping above a barn in Switzerland to walking in the vineyards near the Denkmal at Heidelberg. When we returned to Oregon and Oregon College, we had a reception to announce our marriage, which had been a private affair in Shirley's parent's backyard a month earlier.

Her father gifted us a lot in Dallas as a wedding present. A small house was constructed on it, finished in early October. It cost $12,500 and had 1200 square feet, which translates to $10 a square foot. It was a bargain, by today's prices. Since it was too small for the combining of two households, we began downsizing by donating goods to agencies that accepted them. Who had the better toaster or set of dishes? The loser's went to the donation pile.

The house was a Golden Home, which was a tract home, but nicely finished. There were three bedrooms and 1 ½ baths. We added a shake roof to make it look more like an Oregon home. The rug was the commonly used shag. We had prune trees in the backyard, left over from an ancient orchard that had been on the land. It was a comfortable house, small but nice. We lived there less than a year before we left for new regions of the world.

Shirley finished her doctorate at Oregon State College in June, 1973. Although she applied and received a job at Linfield College [254] in McMinnville, we decided it was the time of our lives to take some risks and try teaching abroad. We interviewed for teaching positions in America Samoa, but that never came to fruition. Vivian A., a recruiter from Adelaide, South Australia, interviewed us both and hired us as secondary teachers. We would immigrate to Australia. I asked for a leave of absence and was granted one from Oregon College. Down under, which we learned not to say, was our next stop.

---

[254] http://www.linfield.edu

Chapter 18   Why Hesitate: Just Emigrate

One of my professors at Portland State had spent time in the U.S.S.R. His perceptions and interpretations of education in another country had always fascinated me. Teaching in Australia would provide a similar experience for me. Shirley and I looked at this as an opportunity to live somewhere else and learn a new culture. She had just finished her doctorate and it was time to take some risks together.

Australia speaks English, but it is not American English. It sounds different and has words that are pronounced and spelled differently. What is a gaol? A tyre? A programme? A controversy? (con-**trav**-a-see) A billabong? What kind of note is a crochet?

And there are three distinct Australian accents, from one similar to the King's English to the outback patois that is difficult to understand.[255] English is not the English we know. We could be understood, but had to be careful talking about our shag rug in Oregon. Shag [256] was a four-letter word for sexual intercourse in Australia.

In August 1973, we were packed and on our way to Adelaide, South Australia, an exciting area in the 1970s.[257] Again, it was a plane, not a train. There are six states in Australia plus ten territories.[258] Tasmania is the only state not connected to the mainland, an island off the southern tip of Victoria State. The country had experienced an influx of immigrants from the U.K., as well as other nations, especially Eastern Europe.[259] They were factory fodder that fueled the growing economy, which boasted only 16,000,000 inhabitants in 1973.[260] An explosion of students intensified the need for teachers, much faster than Australian colleges of advanced education could churn them out. What did the nation do? It outsourced their training to other countries, particularly the United States, and imported teachers to fill the gap. We were part of the gap fillers.

---

[255] http://dialectblog.com/2011/07/10/types-of-australian-accents/
[256] http://www.thefreedictionary.com/shag
[257] http://www.adelaidenow.com.au/news/south-australia/picture-special-everyday-life-in-adelaide-and-south-australia-in-the-1970s/story-fni6uo1m-1227032041047?sv=7a6d344eef9d1eaffc94f4ca3946bb72
[258] https://en.wikipedia.org/wiki/States_and_territories_of_Australia
[259] http://www.australia.gov.au/about-australia/australian-story/changing-face-of-modern-australia-1950s-to-1970s
[260] http://populationpyramid.net/australia/2015/

In those years, there was fear of the "yellow peril",[261] the invasion of Asians. Americans were welcome, Asians, not so much. This changed in the next decades, as refugees arrived from all regions of South Asia. One did not want to buy an Asian car, like a Datsun or Toyota in those earlier years. Buy Australian. Buy a Holden. This was strange to us, given the proximity of the continent to the Asian mainland.

Our plane took us from Portland to San Francisco, and then to Fiji, where we vacationed a few days. The next stop was Sydney on Quanta's and finally Adelaide, South Australia via TAA (Trans-Australian Airlines). We were met by Vivian A. and billeted in a guesthouse on the beach, along with fifteen other American teachers. It had been a luxurious hostel in earlier days but was by now showing the ravages of too many guests and too few renovations.

It was close to the ocean and seemed like a New Jersey resort to us. August is the start of spring in Australia, so we could spend some time on the beach. We had two weeks to acclimate before we would begin teaching. This meant renting a flat, which we did for $35 a week in Lockleys,[262] a suburb of Adelaide. It was small but we felt it was the right price in the right location. The next project was to purchase a car, a new 1973 Torana Holden [263] coupe, blue in color sans heater and radio. The price was $3000 Australian. We financed the car, thinking we would purchase Australian goods with Australian dollars, which made good financial sense.

There were meetings with all the new American teachers in our group to learn of assignments. Many were first year teachers. Others had families with children. It was a "trapped in the elevator" syndrome, knowing we would need each other in the next two or more years since we were expatriates in a foreign land. But the spirit of adventure was high because of a new job in a new country.

Australians told us they liked the English, but not Americans. In reality, we discovered it was exactly the opposite. They seemed to like English ways, systems, government and Brit reserve, but really disliked individual English people. They derogatorily referred to the English as "POMs",[264] which translates as "prisoners of mother England." This slang usage was as old as the British custom of transporting prisoners to Australia in the early 1800s. By contrast, they did not like American ways, our glibness, lack of reserve, brightly colored clothes and ease in

---

[261] https://en.wikipedia.org/wiki/Yellow_Peril
[262] https://en.wikipedia.org/wiki/Lockleys,_South_Australia
[263] https://en.wikipedia.org/wiki/Holden_Torana
[264] http://www.urbandictionary.com/define.php?term=pome

social situations, but really liked individual Americans. We were treated well and we were called "Yanks", even the teachers from the Southern United States.

Australians would ask us if we had met Elvis Presley or knew Elizabeth Taylor. "Have you seen Mickey Mouse?" was common as was: "Do you all carry guns in a holster in America?" (What would they say now?)

Shirley and I were assigned to different high schools.[265] I went to Taperoo, she to Salisbury. They were across the city from each other. Mine was a composite of native-born Australians, but also many students newly arrived from Yugoslavia and Poland. Her students consisted mostly of English immigrants.

It was eye opening to return to high school teaching after five years in a college setting. The classes were huge and all students wore uniforms. Andrea W., the senior or department head, assigned my music courses. Some classes were general music, others prep classes for leaving and matriculation exams. Students who aspired to tertiary education had to matriculate,[266] that is, sit for and pass an exam in six subjects. Music could be one of the subjects. There was no school band or chorus, no performing groups.

I somewhat enjoyed being in a secondary classroom again, but did not see teaching at this level for the two years we had planned to remain in Australia. Discipline was difficult with large classes. It was permissible to use or recommend corporal punishment should a student be consistently disruptive. Punishment was caning, hitting the back of the palm with a stick or ruler.[267] It was typically administered by the head master or assistant head master. I never recommended it and dealt with discipline problems myself. Kids can be unruly, regardless where one is teaching, and verbal reprimands often work. There were times, however, when I considered the "caning" option.

The sociology of the faculty room was interesting, but not conducive for being integrated. Set tables "belonged" to certain teachers and one was told: "That seat is reserved" if you violated their space. Senior teachers (department heads) received deference. As much as I could, I avoided the faculty room and gatherings. After all, I was an American and more than once in Australia, I was informed that American Ph.D.'s are considered cheap degrees compared to a "real" degree earned at an Australian university.

---

[265] http://www.adelaidebound.com/schools.html
[266] https://en.wikipedia.org/wiki/Matriculation
[267] https://en.wikipedia.org/wiki/Caning

A great deal of teaching was rote memorization, neither critical thinking nor problem solving. This was undoubtedly due to the format of the matric exams, which demanded regurgitation of facts and formulas, rather than application and analysis. "Parity of esteem" [268] is a British concept that purports various schools and training programs are all equal in recruitment and social importance, but that proved more fictional than factual. There was a sharp distinction in Australia whether one went to a teachers' college or a university, whether one had a leaving certificate or had matriculated.

That first November in Australia, which was mid-summer, we American teachers were dismayed that there was no Thanksgiving holiday. Aussies do not celebrate American holidays so it was teaching school as usual. Many of us gathered to celebrate the following Saturday, but turkeys were hard to find and anemic compared to Butterballs. Excursions were planned for all the American teachers from time to time, sometimes during the week, other times on weekends. A favorite field trip was to the Barossa Valley, [269] where some of the finest wines in the world are produced. We still search for Australian vintages when we are in a wine shop.

I was asked to present at an in-service for Adelaide music teachers at Raywood, a retreat area. I had mentioned something about related arts on my vita and organizers assumed I was an expert on integrating all the arts in a single course. This was to include music, visual arts and movement. I certainly was not an expert but I became one quickly, researching the typical three strategies for integrating the arts, through common theme, chronology or similar elements.[270] With Shirley's help, I produced a pretty good presentation using 35 mm slides and cassette tapes.

This fluke of the invitation was fortuitous. It would garner me a job at The University of Arizona in a few years, which lasted for 28 years. Lesson learned: Go the extra mile because you may reap unforeseen benefits in the future, beyond your wildest dreams.

By Christmas, Shirley and I had both landed positions in tertiary institutions, she at the Adelaide College of Advanced Education and I at

---

[268] http://www.oxfordreference.com/view/10.1093/oi/authority.20110803100306642

[269] http://us.southaustralia.com/regions/barossa.aspx

[270] http://eric.ed.gov/?id=EJ493891

Torrens College of Advanced Education.[271] Both were teachers' colleges. Mine was a commuter campus. Many of the classes were held in late afternoon or evening. Teachers already in the field were returning to finish a three-year diploma or to earn an advanced diploma, which would qualify them for an administrative position. New students received free instruction but were bonded for three years following course completion. They were required to teach for three years wherever they were placed by the education department, whether in the outback or a predominantly immigrant school.

There was pressure to produce teachers because they were in demand in a country where the population was swelling through immigration. No one failed. If you began a class 30 cohorts, it meant you needed 30 teachers at the end of three years. If someone failed, they were given an extra project to bring him or her to standard.

Shirley's parents, Al and Lydia Q. came for a visit at Christmas. We had a two-week holiday. Christmas dinner was held at a Wildlife Reserve near Adelaide, where a hungry emu pecked into Lydia's fruitcake. Most of us considered it not a big loss. As we know, there is only one fruitcake in the world, and people keep sending it to different households each season. It was the emu's turn.

We drove to Sydney, stopping in Melbourne on the way. I visited the National Gallery[272] and viewed works of Australian artists, including Drysdale[273] and Nolan,[274] the latter of whose paintings of Ned Kelley,[275] an Australian "Billy the Kid", were haunting. In Sydney, we obtained last minute tickets to *The Magic Flute*[276] at the newly opened Opera House.[277] Queen Elizabeth II had dedicated it only two months earlier.[278] Jørn Utzon's architectural marvel, the Sydney Opera House, was highly controversial for years. Its clamshell design against the blue waters of Sydney harbor has since become the symbol of Australia. The acoustics were excellent and Papageno and Papagena's duet[279] memorable.

---

[271] https://www.adelaide.edu.au/records/archives/guide/0857.htm
[272] http://www.ngv.vic.gov.au
[273] http://adb.anu.edu.au/biography/drysdale-sir-george-russell-12439
[274] http://nga.gov.au/COLLECTIONS/AUSTRALIA/GALLERY.cfm?DisplayGal=13
[275] http://www.australia.gov.au/about-australia/australian-story/ned-kelly
[276] ww.britannica.com/topic/The-Magic-Flute
[277] http://www.australia.gov.au/about-australia/australian-story/sydney-opera-house
[278] http://www.history.com/this-day-in-history/sydney-opera-house-opens
[279] https://www.youtube.com/watch?v=OL7YF0Djruk

Visiting museums was part of my plan since I immersed myself in Australian culture, reading books by Patrick White [280] and listening to the music of Peter Sculthorpe. [281]

Every state in Australia was vying for the best performance center. In Adelaide, the Festival Theatre Centre [282] was opened in 1973, where we saw several operas and plays, including some excellent Gilbert and Sullivan. Perth built a center for the arts about the same time. [283] Between 1972 and 1975, the Labor Party, under Prime Minister Geogh Whitlam, [284] was in control in Canberra, the capital. More socialistic than the Liberal Party, which really was "conservative", money flowed for the arts, education and buildings in which they would occur.

New schools were built, many on the open-concept, that is, not as a series of classrooms but with open spaces for integrating the learning across grades and disciplines. We were told many times by Aussies that they were not equal in educational innovation and progress with the United States, but in many ways, during the 1970s they were a step or several steps ahead of us. Perhaps when you are isolated as they thought they were, you try harder. With the Internet active across the globe now, there is no such thing as isolation.

After touring Sydney, we put the in-laws on a plane back to the U.S. and said goodbye. Our next meeting with them would be eighteen months later in Tel Aviv, Israel. We drove back in the Torana through Victoria and flooded areas outside Melbourne to our flat in Lockleys to begin jobs at the tertiary level.

There were only five of us in the music department of Torrens School of Advanced Education, Pat. H., who was chair, plus Viv, Brian and Di. I was assigned the second year music students and was responsible for teaching music theory and history, so it would tie in with their performance study. It was Comprehensive Musicianship, similar to the Ford Foundation project [285] in the U.S., but I did not know it at the time. The class was diverse in ages, some older than I and some much younger. They were eager learners and fun to teach. There were no disparaging remarks about American degrees with this group. They fully accepted me as a viable educator and professional. I was treated well and highly respected, both as a teacher and a musician.

---

[280] http://www.goodreads.com/author/show/50783.Patrick_White
[281] https://en.wikipedia.org/wiki/Peter_Sculthorpe
[282] https://en.wikipedia.org/wiki/Adelaide_Festival_Centre
[283] https://en.wikipedia.org/wiki/Perth_Concert_Hall_(Western_Australia)
[284] https://en.wikipedia.org/wiki/List_of_Prime_Ministers_of_Australia
[285] https://en.wikipedia.org/wiki/Contemporary_Music_Project

Shirley and I traveled every time we had a vacation, which included a guided camping excursion in the Flinders Ranges. [286] The second Christmas, we drove to Brisbane and then down the eastern coastline to Melbourne. In Mallacotta, on the coastline of Victoria, we walked along a road one night and heard a kookaburra.[287] Everyone knows the song, "Kookaburra sits in the old gum tree", but few have heard this raucous, almost primeval bird call in the native environment. It was haunting.

There was an excursion to Alice Springs, [288] which is in the center of the country and Ayers Rock, [289] a sacred symbol to the Aborigines, which I climbed. The best trip, however, was the ISME (International Society of Music Educators[290]) Conference in Perth, which is in Western Australia, on the Indian Ocean.

We took the train from Adelaide across the Nullarbor Plain, [291] which means "no trees". It means almost "no" anything, except kangaroos and wallabies. A lot of time was spent in the club car with friends from Adelaide, sharing a brandy dry over some piano music and songs. It took three days and two nights to cross the continent, but we had a sleeping birth. The trains in Australia never agreed on a common gauge, so we had to de-train outside of Perth and board another train on the outskirts of the city.

After the Raywood Conference, Andrea, my senior at Taperoo, had suggested I submit a presentation idea to the ISME panel months before the conference. I was certainly pleased when I learned my paper was accepted but fully elated when I discovered it would be a plenary session, one that all conferees would see and hear. It had to be something spectacular with an audience that big.

A historical note: We were standing on the steps of the Perth Centre just before the presentation when an Australian friend said to us: "Did you hear? Nixon just resigned as President." [292] Nixon was now history. My presentation was not.

---

[286] http://www.britannica.com/place/Flinders-Ranges
[287] https://en.wikipedia.org/wiki/Kookaburra
[288] http://www.australia.com/en/places/alice-springs.html
[289] http://uluru-australia.com/about-ayers-rock/
[290] http://www.isme.org
[291] http://www.australia.com/en-us/itineraries/crossing-nullarbor.html
[292] https://www.washingtonpost.com/wp-srv/national/longterm/watergate/articles/080974-3.htm

Shirley and I crafted an audio-visual presentation that incorporated slides, music and poetry, based largely on Australian examples. My presentation was very successful and I received a standing ovation. Soon after, I met Bob W., director of The University of Arizona School of Music. We received an invitation to a cocktail party in one of the downtown hotels, where we met Mike H. and Ellie and John B., all faculty members at the UA. "Would I be interested in a job there in a year or so, teaching what I had just demonstrated?" How strange. Nixon was flying out of Washington and we were contemplating a flight to Tucson.

For the next year, letters traveled from Bob W. to me and back about a position available in August 1975. We did not telephone, because the time difference was difficult. I volunteered to return to the U.S. for an interview, but that was never required. I obtained the job at the UA sans interview, affirmative action or a contract. I held three jobs at this point in time. I resigned my position at Oregon College, where I was on leave of absence, as well as Torrens College in Australia.

There were many aspects of living in Australia for almost two years that were quite different from America. Shopping was difficult because stores were open 9-5 during the week and only to noon on Saturday. It was hard to keep groceries in a flat. The fridges were small, so stocking up was not easy. The typical Australian Mum stayed at home and shopped daily. Radios and televisions (black and white) had to be licensed by the government. We were told that official cars drove around checking on signals at each house. You would be fined if you did not have a license for each device. Fact or fiction, we never learned.

Dinnertime was late and if invited to a dinner party that began at 8 p.m., you would be violating protocol if you showed up earlier than 9 p.m. And we were often the first guests, in spite of this. And the evening could go on until 2-3 a.m., about the time the milkman was delivering milk. Yes, we did have milk delivered and it came in liter bottles. Australia began to adopt the metric system a few years earlier, [293] (1968) so we were always mentally converting temperature, distance, volume and weight. But not time.

Speaking of Australian time, [294] we were 17 hours and 30 minutes ahead of the Oregon. (Actually six hours and 30 minutes earlier, but the next day.) If we wanted to call either set of parents, we would call at 10 a.m. on Sunday and they would pick up at 4:30 p.m. the Saturday before. We did telephone from time to time, but it was hard to coordinate

---

[293] https://en.wikipedia.org/wiki/Metrication_in_Australia
[294] https://en.wikipedia.org/wiki/Time_in_Australia

schedules, since Australia is west of the International Date Line,[295] which moves it a day forward. If one travels west, time moves earlier until the Date Line, which simply jumps it to same time next day.

Kangaroos and wallabies existed in profusion in the wild. If one were traveling on a back road, it was good to have a "roo-guard"[296] on your car. We counted numerous dead animals alongside the road on a trip from South Australia to Queensland. Another fear was a pebble on the road hitting your windscreen. It would shatter because the windscreens were not safety glass. We were told to place our hand against the glass when a car was approaching to prevent this calamity. Much like the radio licenses, we were never certain this was truth or folklore, but the shattered glass along the road may have attested to the former.

Cars seldom had heaters in them and air conditioning in an auto was almost unheard of in the 1970s. General Motors, using the molds, chasses, engines and transmissions of American cars, produced Holden cars. Shirley's 1962 EK Holden[297] was much like a 1957 Chevrolet with sturdier suspension for Australian back roads, sans fins. She used it all over the South Australian outback to visit student teachers, including Whyalla.

When Aussies sang:

Once a jolly swagman (traveler)
Sat beside the billabong (lake)
Under the shade of the coolibah (gum) tree
And he sang as he sat
And waited by the billabong (lake)
You'll come a waltzing Matilda (swag or backpack)
With me. [298]

It was more like a hymn, solemn and slow, not fast and frivolous.

Aussies are ostensible Royalists.[299] When Princess Anne[300] and Captain Mark Phillips visited a hospital where our landlady worked, we, too, stood on the sidewalk for a glimpse of her. We also stood on the street

---

[295] http://www.timeanddate.com/time/dateline.html
[296] https://en.wiktionary.org/wiki/kangaroo_bar
[297] http://www.holden.org.au/model/ek-holden/
[298] http://www.kidsongs.com/lyrics/waltzing-matilda.html
[299] https://en.wikipedia.org/wiki/Royalist
[300] http://www.biography.com/people/princess-anne-9185798

another time to view Prince Philip [301] passing in his Rolls Royce limo. Although independent of Mother England and now part of the Commonwealth, [302] the emotional and cultural tie to the United Kingdom was inexorable.

We moved from Lockleys to Rostrevor, [303] an upscale suburb in the hills above Adelaide. Dr. and Mrs. B. were going on sabbatical to Oxford and needed house sitters. They charged the same $35 a week we had paid at Ruth and Jenny's, our former landladies, but we had to endure construction while a wing was added. It was an architecturally designed house, large great room and kitchen with slate floors throughout. No central heating, nor AC, but there was a circulating heater built into the great room. It had three bedrooms and two more were going to be added.

The location was tranquil, next to the Rostrevor Reserve, a natural and protected park, far from city traffic. There frequently were galahs [304] and other exotic birds in our backyard. I moved the old upright piano I had purchased at Lockleys into the great room. I had refinished it in ebony and it made an aristocratic statement in the house. It was a great place to entertain and we hosted frequent dinner parties, including several American teachers the second Thanksgiving, that is, on the following Saturday. Australians never could understand our love of that particular holiday, but we Yanks were not certain about Anzac Day, [305] which is April 25, or Boxing Day, [306] December 26, for that matter. And whoever is Father Christmas? [307] That's just Santa Claus.

The biggest surprise of our Australian adventure came a few days before we were scheduled to leave for Arizona. Australia was socialized, which included medicine and social welfare. Marginal income tax rates were high, [308] absorbing a hunk of our salaries each pay period. If we were able to save any Australian dollars, we transferred them back to the U.S., where the exchange rate was 1 Australian dollar = c. 1.5 U.S. dollars.[309] Transfer $1000 in 1974 and it became almost $1500 in the homeland. We were told that if we exited Australia before two years, our tax dollars would be returned, although we were quite dubious about this actually

---

[301] https://en.wikiquote.org/wiki/Prince_Philip,_Duke_of_Edinburgh
[302] http://thecommonwealth.org/member-countries
[303] https://en.wikipedia.org/wiki/Rostrevor,_South_Australia
[304] https://en.wikipedia.org/wiki/Galah
[305] http://www.australia.gov.au/about-australia/australian-story/anzac-day
[306] http://www.whychristmas.com/customs/boxingday.shtml
[307] http://resources.woodlands-junior.kent.sch.uk/customs/xmas/santa.html
[308] https://en.wikipedia.org/wiki/Income_tax_in_Australia
[309] http://www.forecast-chart.com/usd-australian-dollar.html

happening. The U.S. did not require us to pay tax because we had been working outside the country for over 18 months.

We had lived in Australia 22 months so we were in the window between not owing U.S. tax [310] and receiving back what had been withheld in Australia.[311] There was paper work to sign and offices to visit. I was certain it was not true. A few days before we were to leave, we both went to the tax office and each received a huge check. In addition, we had sold many household goods and accumulated vacation and sick day pay at our schools. There was a pot of money.

As we left the tax office, we were certain someone was going to stop us or pull us into another room, possibly question and even arrest us. That did not happen. We went straight to our bank and had the money transferred to our U.S. accounts. It was a windfall, totally unplanned and unexpected, but it gave us a financial leg up when we returned to the United States in a few months. Where could you go for a couple of years, have unusual and fascinating experiences and receive a windfall like this upon leaving the host country?

There was a crowd of Americans and Australians who saw us off in June 1975 from the Adelaide Airport. We traveled with a combination of Australian dollars, U.S. dollars and German marks. Only the currency of the U.S. was accepted in most places and we eventually returned to our own country with a surfeit of the other two currencies. Whether the American abroad is "ugly" or not, his or her currency always seems to be welcome, even now in contemporary Europe where the Euro, ostensibly, rules.

Our plan was an extensive trip back to the United States through Asia, the Middle East, Europe and then the U.S. First stop was Bali, where we stayed in a luxury hotel and took in the beauty of the island. A peak experience was an evening performance of the Ketjak, a dance of exorcism depicting a battle with monkey soldiers from the Ramayana.[312] I had read about this event and it was well worth experiencing it in its original setting. From here, we flew to Jogjakarta, on the island of Java. A driver picked us up and took us to Salatiga.[313] It had been arranged for me to lecture on related arts at the University of Satya Wacana.[314]

---

[310] https://www.irs.gov/Individuals/International-Taxpayers/Foreign-Earned-Income-Exclusion---Physical-Presence-Test
[311] http://www.elodge.com.au/etax-au/can-claim-100-taxes-back-leave-australia/#.Vikw28u4lZI
[312] https://en.wikipedia.org/wiki/Kecak
[313] https://en.wikipedia.org/wiki/Salatiga
[314] http://www.uksw.edu/en.php

English is spoken but the official language of the country is Bahasa Indonesia.[315] Everything I said was translated sentence by sentence into Bahasa. If I said something humorous, I got two responses.

Salatiga was primitive but the food was delicious, if spicy, even when we had to pick the bugs out of the rice. Bathing was done in a large room with a big cement container of cold water. We were advised: "Do not get into the water." Rather, you took a pitcher to wet yourself, soaped up and then rinsed with the pitcher. It worked but with the high humidity, there was no point in drying off. You would be soaked again in a few moments. Javanese teachers we met used English that sounded as if it had been learned from a tape or "Dick and Jane books". They all wanted to practice their English on American visitors. Indonesia is a country I would like to visit once again. It was charming.

Another peak experience in Salatiga was an evening of Wayang Kulit,[316] which is shadow puppetry. The stories are long but basically depict the battle between good and evil, with puppets of the "right" (literally, the right side of the stage) or "good" ultimately winning. The characters depicted in Wayang Kulit, and they were numerous, are well known throughout the culture, much like our children know Donald Duck, Spiderman or Sponge Bob Square Pants.

On Java, we visited Borobudur, a massive Buddhist shrine, and climbed to the top to view the numerous stupas.[317] Borobudur is considered one of the greatest monuments in the world.

Then it was Bangkok, Thailand, with tours to the Imperial Palace and the upper country, followed by Singapore. We ate in the open market and lived to tell it. Next stop was Delhi, where we took a taxi to Agra to see the Taj Mahal.[318] It was marvelous but hard to move around because Indian children harassed us for money every time we emerged from our hotel. From there we went to Bombay (Mumbai), which was incredibly crowded. India seemed to have rules that changed every time you wanted something, particularly with currency transactions.

We both agreed India was not a good experience so booked a flight out early, landing overnight in the airport at Tehran. I remember the weather in India was humid with lots of storms, typical of their monsoon season. We were not able to hear any authentic Indian ragas in our stay, but there was a profusion of pop music. That was disappointing. Much

---

[315] https://en.wikipedia.org/wiki/Indonesian_language
[316] http://minyos.its.rmit.edu.au/~dwa/WayangKulit.html
[317] http://www.buddhanet.net/boro.htm
[318] http://whc.unesco.org/en/list/252

like our own musical preferences in the U.S., few people in India hear and enjoy classical music.

By this time on this long journey, it had become: "Tuesday. It must be Tel Aviv." And it was. We arrived earlier than our reservations had indicated but found a small room. A few days later, our hotel reservation was available and we met Al and Lydia to continue traveling through Europe. Most of the later trip became a whirlwind, trying to absorb too much culture in too short a time.

But it was still memorable, including a few days at a Kibbutz [319] in Israel, swimming in the Dead Sea and touring the Qumran [320] caves and the Dome of the Rock [321] on Temple Mount. This site is sacred to three religions, Judaism, Christianity and Islam. We saw the site in Bethlehem where Jesus is said to have been born, [322] walked the Via Dolorosa [323] in Old Jerusalem and I left a prayer at the Wailing Wall.[324] Shirley and I risked a dinner in the Old City, cooked by an Arab chef, and lived to tell it. Although not a Victorian nobleman accomplishing his prerequisite Grand Tour, [325] I certainly was able to see places of which I had only dreamed. The train from Mosier indeed led somewhere and I was now in that magical somewhere.

The touring party moved on to Athens, Delphi, Rome, Paris and finally London. We were all tired and ready to go home. We arrived back in Portland the middle of August and spent a brief time with my parents in Mosier. Our household goods, packed in two shipping crates in Australia, had arrived. We gathered what might be needed in Tucson, packed our suitcases and caught a plane to the Old Pueblo.[326]

At this point, one week before the start of classes, I did not even have a contract with The University of Arizona and Shirley had no job at all. It was an act of faith to head to the desert Southwest. However, we would spend the next 28 years at the University of Arizona and then retire in Tucson as well. Although it was a big risk, it was a very wise move, in retrospect, since Tucson has been our home since 1975.

---

[319] http://kibbutzprogramcenter.org/about-kibbutz/
[320] http://www.deadseascrolls.org.il/learn-about-the-scrolls/discovery-sites?locale=en_US
[321] http://domeoftherock.net
[322] http://whc.unesco.org/en/list/1433
[323] http://www.biblewalks.com/Sites/ViaDolorosa.html
[324] http://domeoftherock.nethttp://domeoftherock.net
[325] https://en.wikipedia.org/wiki/Grand_Tour
[326] http://jimturnerhistorian.org/how_the_old_pueblo_got_its_name

Chapter 19   Redefinition: A 28-Year Objective

Tucson was the moon, that is, so seemed its landscape. Neither of us had ever been there before. As we flew into Tucson International Airport, it seemed so dry after the green of Oregon. Not only was it dry, it was very hot. Tucson receives an average of 11.3 inches [327] of rain a year, the largest portion coming during summer monsoons. The average high is 83.7°F, but for summer months it is 100°F. [328] And this was August.

We rented a small car at the airport and headed to a motel we had reserved. The following day, we found the University of Arizona, not that it was to be missed. It was huge, 380 acres [329] near the center of the city, enrolling around 29,000 students. [330] (It currently enrolls over 42,000!) I had wanted to teach at a large university and this was huge, far beyond what I had imagined. I checked out the Music School and picked up my contract from Bob W., which, fortunately, was waiting in my mailbox at the department. Then we hunted for an apartment. It was Saturday and I did not need to report until Monday.

With our furniture still in Dallas, Oregon, we needed something furnished. And we found Villa Serenas, far east on Broadway. It was a place for winter visitors, replete with palm trees, spa and pool. It would work until we found a place to purchase, which was our intent. We cranked down the AC to stay cool.

On Monday, I was welcomed to the UA School of Music along with several other new faculty members. The post-war faculty was reaching retirement age and a new crop of wannabes was arriving. I was assigned three music appreciation classes for the general university student. All classes were held in the recital hall and there were several hundred students in each section. It was a big job. Most students simply wanted an "A" from me without hassle or challenge since this was not a class in their major, but, rather part of their general education requirement.

I tried to integrate music with the other arts, the *raison d'état* for which I had been hired. Apparently the class had been a cakewalk with earlier instructors so I was fighting the "mickey mouse" course image once again when I tried to provide substance and challenge. I had one teaching assistant who handled grading. Although tests were machine scored, I required an individual project from each student. This was sheer

---

[327] http://rainfall.weatherdb.com/l/28/Tucson-Arizona
[328] http://www.usclimatedata.com/climate/tucson/arizona/united-states/usaz0247
[329] https://en.wikipedia.org/wiki/University_of_Arizona
[330] http://oirps.arizona.edu/files/Student_Demo/enrollment_old_current.pdf.

madness on my part, given I had over fifteen hundred students. In order to learn students' names, I requested a note card with a picture (for extra points), so I could post all the cards on my office board and memorize names. At times, for therapy, I was tempted to throw darts at these pictures. But I was successful in learning most of their names. It may have been one of the few times in a large university class that a professor knew the students' names.

The mark of success was the department head had few complaints, at least fewer than in the past. I was pronounced reasonably competent if not highly successful. As in many things in my life, I muddled through, picking up an additional course in music education in the spring semester. Four courses a semester at a research university were unheard of, a teaching overload with grunt labor, once again.

Politics were alive and well in the School of Music. Unlike Oregon College, the University of Arizona School of Music was a conservatory. Studios reigned and teachers competed with one another to attract the best performance students. Many of the faculty members had a world-class reputation. If they had not given a solo recital at Carnegie Hall, they had sung the lead in *La Giaconda* [331] in New York or soloed with the Minneapolis Symphony. [332] And they let you know. Although I really felt out of my league, I did what I was hired to do. For 28 years, more or less, I kept teaching some form of general education course in music for the general university student. My large classes provided a buffer for under-enrolled studios, since each professor was supposed to support 22 full time students (FTE). [333] I was the ostensible cash cow for the School.

Shirley, sans job in Tucson, pounded the pavement and found classes to teach at Pima Community College [334] as well as the School of Education at the University of Arizona. The following year, she interviewed and achieved a position in Cooperative Extension in the College of Agriculture, which would eventually lead to an administrative position covering the entire state of Arizona. She traveled the state as a Human Development Specialist. I would accompany her if possible and we came to know most regions of Arizona, including the three Native American reservations, Navajo, Hopi and Apache, as well as many of the small Arizona towns.

The School of Music was not particularly a friendly place. It was so big I did not know everyone on the faculty, not to mention the numerous

---

[331] https://en.wikipedia.org/wiki/La_Gioconda_(opera)
[332] https://en.wikipedia.org/wiki/Minnesota_Orchestra
[333] https://en.wikipedia.org/wiki/Full-time_equivalent
[334] https://www.pima.edu

graduate teaching assistants who were affiliated with instruction. In a large university, a professor is his or her own boss, teaching classes, when assigned, but largely accomplishing research or concertizing around the world. A reputation is earned in that manner, which builds a case for eventual tenure consideration. I wrote articles for national publications, but I was not conducting research like those in the science or social sciences. Nonetheless, I did publish. The paradigm was shifting in higher education. Teaching was no longer the primary goal, research was.

When it came time for a tenure decision, I made it without a problem. This was not the same when I applied for a full professorship. Not enough research and publishing. Too young. Need more of everything. Need to wear a suit to work. Promotions had no financial advantage. In the School of Music, most promotions were titular and dry, that is, no salary boost.

I became interested in textbook publishing, which helped with tenure. At Oregon College, Alice K. and Dick B. had built a national reputation on their publications. Since I incorporated music of other cultures in my teaching, it was a natural to produce a small book on listening to music of India, Indonesia and Japan. Kendall Hunt,[335] a small company which specialized in textbooks designed for a particular course, published it. The title was: *Non-Western Music and the Western Listener* and it is still available on Amazon.com, [336] although it was originally published in 1977. Kendall Hunt required the author to provide typed copy with all visuals ready to insert. It was little more than "self-publication", but they did provide typeset page proofs.

During one break, we took a short vacation to Bahia Kino in Sonora and I used that time to proof read and make final corrections. It was exciting to realize I would have a book in print and that it might help me attain tenure. It did. My boss, however, never referred to it as book. To him, it was always a booklet. However, it was 107 pages and it would be the first of thirteen books I would eventually write.

A large land-grant university is quite different from a small liberal arts or teachers' college. Research rules. Professors would write grants to enhance their salary and even buy themselves out of teaching. This was particularly true in the sciences, where salary funds were connected to large grants. This was not possible in music or the arts, but the

---

[335] https://www.linkedin.com/company/kendall-hunt-publishing-company

[336] https://books.google.com/books/about/Non_western_music_and_the_western_listen.html?id=Mr8ZAQAAIAAJ

standard was similar across campus. Enhance your department and your career by bringing in external dollars.

Students were equally different. At Oregon College, many students were first-generation college and had great hope and faith in upward mobility through higher education. Professors were respected. At the UA, many students had parents who had graduated prestigious universities and were lawyers, doctors, and CEOs. Respect for teachers was correspondingly different, more the role of a servant than a curator of learning. Although the cost of tuition for 1975 is not available, in 1987, in-state tuition was $1136, out-of-state, $4260.[337] (For 2015, it is $11,400 and $32,600, respectively.[338]) As state funding declined, tuition costs rose. It took money to attend The University of Arizona, even with financial aid. Many students had the attitude: "I'm buying this and I will tell you what I want", a stance not aided by the notion of student as customer, rather than, student as learner. Parents tended to support this notion.

Equally perplexing was the use of one's textbook in one's class. Some students believed it was unfair to require the professor's book in a class in which they were enrolled. This was putting money into the professor's pocket at the expense of students, even when the book was used at numerous other universities around the country. To the contrary, students would also complain if a different text were used that did not follow the professor's lectures. It was an interesting conundrum that had no solution. The University pretty well looked the other way on the issue and textbook production was common.

In my years at the University of Arizona, I produced additional texts that were widely adopted around the United States, including *Teaching Music*, with Holt, Rinehart and Winston, *Creative Music Fundamentals*, with Prentice-Hall, *The Listening Experience* (1st and 2nd edition with Schirmer-MacMillan Music) and *Music in World Cultures* (Kendall Hunt) [339] plus accompanying teachers' texts. All of these texts are now out of print. In the age of eBooks and streaming music, hardcopy textbooks have ceased to be important. For me, however, I achieved status as an author and teacher, which led to presentations at conferences and in-services around the country. The royalties that came in were never extensive, but were adequate enough for special purchases in our household, which our

---

[337] http://www.collegecalc.org/colleges/arizona/university-of-arizona/
[338] https://financialaid.arizona.edu/undergraduate/2015-2016-estimated-cost-attendance
[339] http://www.amazon.com/James-Patrick-OBrien/e/B001HOPIO6/ref=ntt_dp_epwbk_0

salaries did not allow. Unfortunately, there was never a correlation between rising tuition costs and faculty salaries.

There was some exciting international travel in our early years at The University of Arizona. In 1980, Shirley and I both traveled to Warsaw to present at ISME (International Society of Music Education). Poland was part of the Soviet Bloc, so we had heightened security when we crossed Checkpoint Charlie [340] and eventually caught a plane to Warsaw. Officials scrutinized our slides at the conference before we were permitted to do our presentations. This was never seen as censorship, but rather a requirement that their equipment be compatible with our material.

A particular highlight of this trip was meeting Dmitry Kabelevsky, Russian composer.[341] Ozan M.,[342] concert pianist on the faculty at Arizona, had premiered one of Kabelevsky's piano concertos and wanted us to deliver a medal and photo, Ozan at the piano, Dmitry standing behind. At the cocktail party in Warsaw, where he was to appear, bodyguards and secret police surrounded Kabelevsky. We approached him, but not close enough to speak. We held up the photo so he could see it and he pushed through right to us. The exchange was brief because he was quickly spirited away, but it was a pretty heady moment to shake hands with such a famous composer.

This tour took us through Poland and Hungary, ending in Austria. The black market was alive and well behind the Iron Curtain. We would place a U.S. $20 bill under our napkin in the hotel restaurant. The napkin would be swept away by the wait staff and replaced with another napkin. There would be Polish zlotys [343] underneath at a much better rate than at an official bank. We were warned we could be arrested for doing this but it never happened. I became the banker for many on the tour who were afraid to try it.

In 1982, we had both been at the University six years so could apply for a sabbatical. A sabbatical is a privilege, not a right, but most faculty in music were easily awarded one if their proposal had good objectives. Mine did. I would study the ethnic music in select countries in Africa. Although Shirley had spent time in Cameroon with her uncle and aunt, who were medical missionaries, I had never traveled to this continent. It was not my first choice for travel. I would have preferred the warm beaches of Puerto Vallarta or Mazatlan. But Africa it was.

---

[340] http://www.dailysoft.com/berlinwall/history/checkpoint-charlie.htm
[341] http://www.britannica.com/biography/Dmitry-Kabalevsky
[342] https://en.wikipedia.org/wiki/Ozan_Marsh
[343] http://www.thefreedictionary.com/zloties

We left our Chihuahua puppy dog, Little Bit, with my parents in Mosier and flew from Portland to London. Then it was London to Lagos, Nigeria,[344] then Enugu, a regional airport. Here we met Shirley's graduate student, Betty I., who was of the Ibo people. We spent a week in a Gasthaus and practically starved to death. There was little food to be had and it was mostly soup with a little chicken (or was it chicken?) The conditions were primitive. No hot water for a bath. There was one restaurant in the Gasthaus, which was very low on food. We were told not to drink the water so were dehydrated and slightly ill most of our stay. Also, we were taking a healthy dose of quinine pills as an antimalarial prophylactic. It was an experience I never care to repeat.

Nigeria is a large country,[345] a third larger than Texas, and it is the most populous country in Africa. When the states of Africa were carved out by colonial powers, warring tribes were kept within the same borders. There are presently 300 different tribes. There has always been conflict among the predominant tribes, Hausa, Ibo and Yoruba, who account for 70% of the population.[346] Oil is king but governmental corruption has tainted the region for decades.

The visit was only a week but it seemed much longer. We finally received an invitation to visit the University at Nigeria at Enugu, since Betty's spouse was a lecturer there. We were invited to a morning gathering with other professors, which included peanuts and whiskey as refreshment. I would have preferred bottled water. Soon we flew back to Lagos and experienced confusion trying to find our plane and board it. We watched as bribes were proffered to flight attendants to allow those without a ticket on the plane. Life was expensive in Nigeria and the poverty overwhelming. But we made it out.

Next stop was Cameroon, where we experienced some native music. We spent time with Presbyterian medical missionaries at Metet as well as with an African family we had met in Canada. Zaire was next on the journey and we spent a full month there. (This is now the Democratic Republic of Congo.[347]) Zaire [348] is a huge country, the third largest in Africa as well as the third most populous. It is one-quarter the size of the U.S. and there are 200 tribes within its borders. Mobutu [349] was in

---

[344] http://www.mapsofworld.com/nigeria/cities/
[345] http://mapfight.appspot.com/texas-vs-ng/texas-nigeria-size-comparison
[346] http://answersafrica.com/nigerian-tribes.html
[347] http://www.bbc.com/news/world-africa-13283212
[348] http://www.nationsencyclopedia.com/economies/Africa/Congo-Democratic-Republic-of-The.html
[349] http://www.britannica.com/biography/Mobutu-Sese-Seko

power and we once saw his motorcade of shiny new Mercedes limousines drive by. We were billeted in a compound in Kinshasa, the capital, and there was a museum, which had numerous musical instruments of the country.

Our travels included flying to other regions with a Mission Aviation Fellowship [350] pilot in a Cessna 180, for a fee, of course. The roads and telephones the Belgians had constructed during the colonial period, were long gone. Travel by auto was impossible. Rich O., our pilot, placed us in his small craft for balanced weight distribution and we flew to Kikwit for a few days, then Tshikapa, followed by Nyanga and finally Kananga. He would land the plane in a field, buzzing it first to clear the cattle. Upon landing, a sea of faces would gather around the plane, arranged by height and age. A single Anglo, usually the missionary, would then welcome us and the crowd would cheer.

As we were in the air on the way to Tshikapa, Rich jokingly said: "Let me know if you see a missile coming toward us." Had we flown over Angola, which shares a border with Zaire, that could have happened. We were actually very close to the border. Mobutu received U.S. support because Angola was backed by the Soviet Union. Had we violated Angolan air space, a missile could have been launched.

We stayed the longest at Nyanga, which was high on a central plateau. It had the most missionaries, principally Mennonite, [351] some single and some married. We were invited to an evening of music at the community center, which was an open pavilion. I hoped finally to see and hear some authentic ethnic music. The Zairian young men, however, showed up in polyester shirts, unbuttoned to the waist, and demonstrated their dance moves like John Travolta to music similar to *Saturday Night Fever*. One enterprising young man shoved a cassette tape of his band into my hand to take back to the U.S. so they could be discovered.

The missionaries were wonderful to us, sharing their faith, skills and food in the community, often at great sacrifice, and asking us to participate in their daily activities. Unlike missionaries of old, they were chosen because they had a skill needed in the country, whether medicine, education or agriculture. Burning passion to save souls was secondary to what the country needed. Their lives were not secure, particularly in Zaire, which was essentially a police state. Food was never plentiful and we estimated most missionaries spent a great amount of time procuring food and trying to stay healthy and clean. The mission job was probably 20% of what they did. And none of it was ever easy.

---

[350] https://en.wikipedia.org/wiki/Mission_Aviation_Fellowship
[351] http://mennoniteusa.org/who-we-are/

The flight back to Kinshasa was in an old DC-3, [352] more suited to the military than civilian air service. The lavatory was a large bucket in the rear of the plane. Since the plane was not pressurized, it was cold. My body told me to divest of liquid, so, consequently, I visited that bucket several times.

Last stop on the sabbatical was Kenya, which seemed cosmopolitan compared to the three other nations we had visited. We stayed with a colleague of our minister, Dr. Joe K., who took us to a Moslem wedding as well as a three-person safari in the bush. We were almost swept away crossing a river on our return to his house. We didn't see any elephants, but we saw their fresh scat and trees they had broken down in search of food.

A tenure of 28 years at one university is a case study in how to stay motivated and vitalized, particularly when the assignment does not change much from year to year and boredom sets in. The challenge of writing a book, which is a boring and lonely process, and travel, which is hard work but never lonely, both wear off. In the next stage of my University of Arizona life, two things happened.

In 1982, I decided to begin an M.B.A. [353] at the College of Business. It did not seem like any conflict of interest because many of the courses were held at night, after my music duties were finished. I applied formally to the Graduate College and took several courses for the next two years, including accounting, business statistics, economics, marketing, finance and management. Although I taught one course for part of the summer, I could still take three business courses towards the degree the rest of the summer. It was a new world to me since many of my fellow students were working in industry. It was a new circle of friends, many of whom knew I was a tenured professor. When we had small groups for a class project, we would use my office to accomplish the planning.

Just as I was completing all the course work, an associate dean in the Graduate College discovered I was a tenured faculty member. There was a rule in the Faculty Handbook that prohibited a tenured professor from receiving an advanced degree from the University. The rule was silly, since I was tenured in music but seeking a degree in business. No conflict of interest there. I tried to appeal it, but to no avail. (The rule no longer exists!)

---

[352] http://www.aviation-history.com/douglas/dc3.html
[353] https://en.wikipedia.org/wiki/Master_of_Business_Administration

The dean of the graduate college said he would work out an exchange with Arizona State University so I could complete the degree there. The deal was struck and all I had to do was take the core M.B.A. courses at A.S.U. It meant attending classes there for two summers and commuting two years during fall and spring semester, which was 110 miles, one way. I survived it and so did Shirley, although it was a strain on our marriage. In December 1986, I was awarded an M.B.A. at Arizona State University. It required twice as much course work as I had taken for my Ph.D. two decades earlier, but it was a new set of skills and understandings. I had hoped it would provide a pathway to an administrative position at the University of Arizona, but that never happened.

I did use the degree to invest our savings wisely, to purchase and sell real estate as licensed agent for 20 years and to work as a tax preparer for Jackson-Hewitt for a few seasons at night. I guess I never wanted to settle on one discipline. I just had too much energy to do or be one thing. I was multi-tasking before the term was used.

The second thing that happened was the personal computer. Jobs and Wozniak invented the first Apple computer in 1976 [354] and the world was now moving from mainframes to personal computers. I wanted one. I had taken a computer class in my M.B.A. studies, but it was using an NCR (National Cash Register) in a computer lab, where we had to write a simple program in BASIC [355] or Beginner's All-purpose Symbolic Instruction Code.

There were some cast-off Franklin Ace 1000 [356] computers in our college and I was given one upon request, my first PC. By today's standards, it was a dinosaur, but I had word processing software for doing my business papers while completing the M.B.A. I even ran a statistics program on the little "A" drive that was attached to it. Later in my career, we would use the Franklins and Apple IIe's as doorstops, but in 1984, this was state of the art. I used an early Macintosh to create listening lessons via CD-ROM with software called HyperCard.[357] Every two or three years, I would write a grant to update my computers and moved through seven or eight generations of Macintosh computers to create courses online. Not only was this readily accepted by students, it became highly profitable.

---

[354] http://inventors.about.com/od/cstartinventions/a/Apple_Computers.htm
[355] https://en.wikipedia.org/wiki/BASIC
[356] http://www.vintage-computer.com/franklin.shtml
[357] http://www.macworld.com/article/2862265/think-retro-how-hypercard-inspired-a-generation-of-future-developers.html

By streaming music online, using mp3s, [358] I was able to create online courses in which students could enroll during semester breaks to pick up extra credits. There was no classroom contact with students in these courses. They existed entirely online and the only contact was email. My last three years at the University, I facilitated these online classes in winter break, for three weeks, after spring semester, for three weeks, and throughout the summer. With dial up email, I could be in contact with my students 24/7.

The thrust of this was that it was supplementary income, outside of my regular contract. In those six weeks of intersession, I doubled my academic salary, shoring up my retirement account. I never dreamed I would be earning six figures as a music professor, but I did the last three years of teaching, thanks to electronic entrepreneurship.

Why did the Music School allow this? It brought in numerous dollars to them as well, revenue from the tuition charged students. No one ever queried my endeavor. I could be in California on vacation while students were taking a test I had posted online, whether they were in Denver, New York, Paris or Tel Aviv. What a bonanza. Not only was I using technology to enhance instruction, but I was growing my retirement annuity as well. This was probably the epitome of my teaching, the ability to deliver instruction and manage it virtually. I also believe this is the total wave of the future. Buildings and classrooms are too expensive to compete with online learning. There are so many courses, which can be done online and music appreciation was one of them.

In my 28 years at the University, I did have two assignments outside the School of Music. One was working as a loaned executive for United Way of Tucson. [359] A Vice President, much higher up than my department chair, who resented that I was being spirited away without his input, made this assignment. A teaching assistant was assigned my classes and I was off to United Way on Speedway Boulevard to raise money for programs in Tucson. It was a productive assignment. There were several young colleagues from Tucson, all loaned executives from Tucson's many businesses or corporations.

My job was to visit a company, such as Brush Wellman, [360] do a presentation to their employees, and then ask for a pledge to United Way be deducted monthly or weekly from their paycheck. I had good response and my best memory of this experience is climbing up a ladder on the factory floor and doing a presentation with a bullhorn. There

---

[358] http://www.webopedia.com/TERM/M/MP3.html
[359] http://www.unitedwaytucson.org
[360] http://www.indeed.com/cmp/Brush-Wellman

must have been 200 employees listening, much like my captive audiences at the University. One also hoped for a sizeable corporate donation after a presentation.

Another diversion was a year working for Extended University, now termed Outreach College.[361] Bill N., a vice president for outreach, bought my contract out for one year and I became a program development specialist. This was merely a fancy name for one who finds instructors and sets up courses, certificates and even degrees in sites off-campus.

My beat included Sierra Vista, where I worked with Cochise College to set up a 2+2 degree program, as well as Casa Grande and Nogales. There were lots of breakfasts with Chamber of Commerce personnel as well as community college administrators. I met a lot of important people in this position. In Tucson, I set up non-credit evening courses in music, film, theatre, dance and the visual arts. Bill was a tough boss, probably the best and most honest one I ever had, and remarked: "You will need to grow your skin thicker if you want to do administration." It was a great year, but I returned to music the following year. My skin was and always will be pretty thin.

Between 1978 and 1995, Shirley and I were ministers of music at the Church of the Painted Hills, [362] a United Church of Christ [363] church on the west side of Tucson. This meant a Wednesday choir practice, preparation of organ/piano duets for the Sunday prelude and offertory, as well as another early practice on Sunday morning, followed by the entire service. It was a hike from our house in Sabino Canyon to Painted Hills, but we did it faithfully for seventeen years, before traffic became an obstacle.

Dr. Joe B. was the pastor when we first came. A University of Chicago graduate, he was elegant and proper, but kind and gentle. He was a pleasure to work with. When he retired, we had Rev. Les S. and then Rev. David C., both of whom looked at religion differently but always effectively. It was a rich time in our lives, serving in church, and making good music. We had great support and even good salaries by the time we said the church needs new blood after seventeen years. And it did. We continue to maintain many friends from that era.

We also moved four times in our working years, from a rented studio apartment at Villa Serenas to a townhouse on River Road. From there,

---

[361] https://oc.arizona.edu
[362] http://www.tobeys.org/cphucc/CPH%20Short%20History.htm
[363] http://www.ucc.org

we moved further north and built a house in Hidden Valley and lived there for ten years. Even further north in the foothills, we built a house in Canyon View Estates. It was a huge house with many amenities, but after seventeen years, when we finally retired and sold it, it needed renovation. Shirley and I have never renovated. We sell and buy a new house. Then we moved even further north to SaddleBrooke, a retirement community, near the little village of Catalina. We always made money on real estate, which was basically true for most people until the crash of 2008.

My years at the University were long, sometimes good and sometimes not so great. There were some effective department heads for the School of Music and then there were some administrative lean years. Leadership could be more striving than succeeding. The pay was the same, regardless, but I do look back at all the bosses and recall that Bob W., the man who hired me in Australia, was the best of all the department heads. He had a global outlook for a department and knew how to balance priorities and manage huge egos. He was the director for ten years of my 28 there but moved on to manage the Cincinnati Conservatory. He could scold without being vindictive, reward without courting one's conceit. I was lucky to have him for a boss.

When I decided to retire from teaching in 2003, Dean Maurice S.,[364] a colorful leader to say the least, asked three retiring professors to deliver the commencement address to the School of Fine Arts graduates. The other two declined, so I was the sole speaker. This is what I said:

I'm honored to be the Commencement speaker tonight.
There are lots of similarities between you graduates and myself . . .
We're all looking at new beginnings.
You're having some fear about the future
AND, so am I

You're exhilarated about the great unknown out there
AND, so am I
You've had a massive case of senioritis this past semester
AND, so did I (Although perhaps it was more like senior moments)

You're 22 or 26 or 30 or 34
AND, I'm not going there.

Let's look at it as if our lives in the arts were a dining experience at a fine restaurant.

---

[364] http://www.artbymaurice.com

*I arrived considerably earlier than you, (40 years to be exact)
And it has been a great meal. . An impeccably fine dining experience. I'm savoring the afterglow.*

For you, having arrived later, you've just finished the euphoria of pre-dinner drinks and are feeling high and perhaps trying to figure out how to pay your bar bill (that is, your student loans) while looking forward now to the main course . . . the main course of life.

*For me, the meal is over.
I'm not coming back to this restaurant
I'm just going to sit back and enjoy some strong coffee and an exquisite dessert . . . I know it's going to be sweet!
Then I'll figure out what I'm going to be when I grow up.*

Now if you want to enjoy your meal, this meal of life in the arts, there are some table manners you might want to be aware of . . . that I'm going to share with you, since you'll be dining long after I've left.

I call these the six principles for successful dining in the Arts

Principle #1: Even though you're in the arts and enjoy your work, remember that accountants, nurses, football coaches, engineers and heart surgeons enjoy their work too . . . those of us in the arts have no monopoly on job satisfaction

Principle #2: Although we're ostensibly the self-nominated creative types, remember those in other professions are just as creative . . . we do it with gesture, color, footage, timing and sound . . . others do it with space shuttles, laparoscopic surgery, cantilevers, video cameras on Abrams tanks, income statements, and MRIs . . . recognize and celebrate creativity whenever you find it . . . it's part of the human condition . . . we have no monopoly on it.

P.S. Thank goodness I have a creative accountant.

Principle #3: Having a degree places you in 25% of the population with privilege . . . that is not license for special treatment. Rather, it is mandate to share that largesse with the other 75% who are also bright and significant and creative. . But just didn't go to college. If you treat people as intelligent beings, you'll not be disappointed.

Principle #4: You may not make lots of money in the arts, but most people in life don't make a lot of money (whatever that means) . . . but earning it year after year in a fulfilling career and managing it wisely is what grows prosperity, not the starting salary in six figures that fizzles the minute the NASDAQ declines.

Principle #5: It is wonderful to be excellent at things . . . but in a world where focused excellence is now a mantra, remember, it is okay to demonstrate diffused mediocrity at many other things . . . you don't have to be perfect at everything. Just strive for reasonable competence and you'll excel.

Principle #6: Never, never give up your art . . . never give up those special skills and aptitudes you have developed for most of your life . . . even if you have a day job or two jobs that pay the bills . . . just get up earlier . . . to practice, to paint, to prepare for that audition, to stretch, to capture the morning light through your lens. . To put your head on correctly.

So savor your meal . . . it is quickly consumed and the plates are removed from the table before you know it . . . my 40+ professional years fairly flew . . . I was born when FDR was in the White House, first voted for a man named JFK, and now a guy with only one initial is the President . . .

Congratulations. You will find your meal at the UA will provide incredible staying power for years to come.
Best wishes for nutritional success and balanced well-being!

With that as my swan song, I retired from the University of Arizona after 28 years, in June 2003, but with 42 years total in the teaching profession. Some colleagues said I was being let out for good behavior. Shirley joined me in that retirement with 43 years. It was time. There was life beyond the job.

Chapter 20   It's A Dog's Life

The story of my life would not be complete without an element, about which I may have alluded but never discussed, at least in detail. The subject is dogs. There have been many writings and studies on the benefit of adding a dog to a family. There are fewer cases of depression among family members. Dog owners have elevated dopamine, [365] lower blood pressure and lower cholesterol levels.[366] The same article alludes to the "touch" factor as a benefit as well. Petting a dog satisfies the need to stroke and massage. Shirley and I always walked our dogs, so there is a cardiovascular advantage as well, not to mention frequent laughter a crazy dog can elicit from its owners.

There were always pets when I was growing up. Tippy is the first family dog I remember, followed by Pal, a talented brown terrier. Pal came to us in Drain and was one of the few dogs, early on, who was allowed in the house, but only as an occasional guest. In cold weather, he would sleep on the open oven door of the wood cook stove. Most of our dogs were small and shorthaired. My parents did not tolerate cruelty to an animal and we were taught to appreciate and love them. Happy, a fox terrier, was with us for twelve years. She was given to us by Fritz F., and lived with us in Hood River, Dallesport and Mosier. I came home from college one weekend in 1961 and my parents said she was gone. It was a sad time. She was a great companion who loved to walk in the woods with me as well as watch the Union Pacific trains with me below our home. She even spent some time with me at my lookout job in Washington, but vanished down the five-mile trail one night. Fortunately, my brother retrieved her and she was returned to my parent's house.

Poco, our beloved chocolate Chihuahua only lived six years. He was the first dog that was allowed to live in the house all the time. Then there was Mopsy, my mother's dog, who bore four pups, Bimbo, Spot, Tip and Blossom. Mom kept all four, until her death in 1987. And Spot outlived Mom and his siblings, passing on at age 17. There is a little cemetery on the Mosier property where these companion animals are all interred. If I am traveling near Mosier on I-84, I always look up at the old house and hope those graves have never been disturbed. But, then, they have already met Mom and Dad and crossed the Rainbow Bridge. [367]

When I was a child, a dog was a dog, not a companion animal. They generally lived and slept outside. Because they rarely were vaccinated

---

[365] https://www.psychologytoday.com/basics/dopamine
[366] http://www.helpguide.org/articles/emotional-health/the-health-benefits-of-pets.htm
[367] http://www.rainbowbridge.com/Poem.htm

for rabies, many lived short lives, ravaged by parvovirus or distemper. Since they were free roamers, a passing auto could easily kill them. Licensing and vaccinations were not common. By comparison, nowadays, dogs are treated much better, receiving regular veterinary care and protection. Since 37-47% of Americans have a dog, [368] this is good news. They live longer and they live better.

In 1979, Shirley and I thought Lydia, who had just lost Al, would like a dog for company. We visited Linda N., a dog-lady for certain, and she had one she thought appropriate. This was Little Bit, a six-pound black-and-tan deer Chihuahua.[369] Linda said she was pure bred, but we suspected a miniature pinscher relative somewhere in the genes. American Kennel Club papers were never proffered and we didn't ask. The dog was outrageous, a total clown. We took her home, waiting for Lydia's next visit to fetch Little Bit. But we fell in love with this dog and decided to keep her. This made no sense at all in our busy lives of teaching, travel, church work and programs of physical fitness. Little Bit became a member of our household for the next eleven years. We had to return to Linda and find a substitute Chihuahua for Lydia, a cubby Chihuahua named Mitzi.

Little Bit's age was unknown, but she did have health problems. Her teeth were bad, but I brushed them anyway. Or I tried. Her nose sloughed off, her anal glands clogged and her eyes were always dry. She was a vet's dream retirement fund but we never balked at expenses. She was worth it. She would travel with us on a plane, secure under our seat in a small carrier. We would usually extract her when the flight attendant was not looking and put her between us, covered with a blanket. Security was looser in those days. She traveled all over Arizona with us in the back seat of the car. When we had longer trips, Linda kept her. During our African sabbatical, she stayed with my parents.

When we left for work in the morning, she would sit on the couch and cry. When we arrived home, she would run back and forth in the halls, squealing with delight. She looked much like Snoopy [370] running in Peanuts or the dachshund in Bella's painting.[371] When we walked after dinner, she stayed beside us and never was leashed. She was a tiny friend, who provided much comic relief for 11 years. After a stroke,

---

[368] https://www.aspca.org/about-us/faq/pet-statistics
[369] https://en.wikipedia.org/wiki/Chihuahua_(dog)
[370] http://www.peanuts.com/characters/snoopy/#.Vi6eddD0jU4
[371] http://www.independent.co.uk/arts-entertainment/art/great-works/great-works-dynamism-of-a-dog-on-a-leash-1912-giacomo-balla-1781174.html

which occurred on the hottest day [372] Tucson had ever recorded, 117 degrees, on June 26, 1990, she went downhill fast. She had been in the garage with plenty of water but never drank water unless we were with her. In September, we put her down. Putting a dog down is one of the saddest things I have ever done, not because your companion animal is gone forever, but that you made the decision to do it.

We were enjoying our sabbatical that year and were spending time researching and writing at our big cabin in Pine, Arizona, about 200 miles north of Tucson. We decided to take a short trip to Spain, only ten days. A few days before leaving, I happened to go by a pet store and checked out the puppies. There were two miniature pinschers, [373] brothers, one red, and one black and tan. I called Shirley to have a look. We both agreed the latter would be our dog. He had been in the store for some time and was deeply discounted to move the merchandise, we always joked. The store agreed to hold him until we returned from Spain.

He was an energetic and peppy little guy. His name, Peppin, came from a contraction of "peppy" and "pinscher". What a dog. When we brought him home, he had never been out-of-doors and ran back and forth in our large backyard. He had never climbed stairs before, so bounced up and down the steps to the yard. Peppin had been in the pet store so long that he had developed a phobia of people coming up to him and poking at the glass. He never lost the phobia. If he were in a car and someone came to the window, he would go berserk. I guess we all have phobias based on the environment in which we are raised, and he was no different.

Peppin attended obedience school and even graduated, but not as head of the class. He did develop competency with commands and learned to walk on a leash so you barely knew he was there. He would automatically sit if you stopped. He was a registered minpin with the AKC [374] and had show qualities. Like many minpins, however, he was fiercely protective, darting at visitors' legs if we did not control him. He was a biter too. We always joked that if we didn't watch him: "Peppin would take someone out for a bite." The most precarious time was selling our big cabin in Pine. The woman who made an offer came by the house with her five-year old granddaughter, who got a bite from Peppin. We thought the deal would fall through and we would be sued. But it

---

[372] http://tucson.com/news/blogs/monsoon/tucson-monsoon-on-this-day-in-tucson-hit-its-hottest/article_92ba854e-bfd7-11e1-84c1-001a4bcf887a.html
[373] http://www.akc.org/dog-breeds/miniature-pinscher/
[374] http://www.akc.org

was just a scrape, not a puncture. We still sold the cabin and Peppin was not quarantined.

Two years later, we decided to add a female minpin to our menagerie. We found a puppy described in an ad in the newspaper and contracted with the breeder to pick her up in a few weeks. She was a tiny little dog and we named her Mindipin. She was a darling, feminine and fun.

Mindipin was prone to accidents and it seems we were always rushing her to the vet. One morning, after an ample breakfast of dry food, suitable for a growing girl-dog, she inadvertently fell into the spa. We were right there to grab her out, but she had taken in water, which made the dry dog food swell in her tummy. A trip to an emergency vet eased our minds. She would have a big tummy ache for about eight hours and everything would pass, literally.

Minpins are jumpers and can spring up like magic to get on a bed, chair or table even. One Saturday morning, Mindipin, not yet six months, jumped on the waterbed. We heard her jump down and cry painfully. Her front leg was broken, hanging limply as we tried to console her. Too much weight for the tiny legs, not fully matured. We rushed to the vet and were certain she would be put down. The doctor said it could be repaired and she went into a delicate surgery, followed by a cast for several weeks. The leg was miraculously repaired and she never limped. Unfortunately, this was in her formative period as an agile dog and she never quite mastered the coordination Peppin developed, struggling at times to jump into a chair or lap. Later, she blew out her knee with more jumping and that required another surgery. Never daunted, she would recover and bring us more joy and delight.

Peppin always asked: "Why did you go muck up my life by buying a dog?" but he had a good relationship with her, after the two became acquainted. In our large living room, one would chase the other. Then, for no reason at all, the chase would be reversed. They would play tug-a-war, growling like twin T-rexes in *Jurassic Park*. And both swam in our pool, Mindipin, willingly, but Peppin, not so much. We taught them both where to swim so if they ever fell into the pool, they could find the stairs and get themselves out. Mindipin would jump in on her own, if I were swimming, but Peppin never did. If separated, they would both kiss noses and whine with noises we only heard when once reunited.

Peppin came into our lives in 1990, soon after we lost Little Bit. Mindipin was two years later. They both loved to travel in a motor home, jumping onto the dash area once we were in port so they could survey the resort and comment on every dog's action, size and attitude. They never were quiet.

We had Peppin until 2006, Mindipin, until a year later. Both were put down because of health reasons. He lived beyond 16 years and she was 14 ½. Peppin could not hear and could not see but we always thought there would be a miraculous renewal. Mindipin's kidneys stopped functioning. We had to "irrigate" her with fluid injections once a day to remove the impurities. It was doggy dialysis and it only worked so long. She was so willing for us to hang the IV, punch her with a needle in the fat behind her neck and let the saving juices flow. But a dog will tell you when it is time to make that fateful trip to the vet. And so we had to eventually do it for both, which never gets easier because you have done it before with a beloved pet. Mindipin sent us a beautiful sunset in Las Vegas the day she departed, which said to us she made it to Rainbow Bridge [375] and was waiting for us. I know there is a heaven and I know my dogs will be part of it. I still tear up when I think of the day we made that last trip to the vet for each.

A new furry life never replaces the one that is gone, but it does help fill the empty space when a beloved pet passes on. Dogs have always been important to me because they provide unconditional love. They are always there for you and they reflect your mood, commiserating or celebrating, when you need it most. Rev. David C., minister at Painted Hills while we were there, said it best: "You come home after a bad day. Your dog meets you at the front door to greet and cheer you. If it really were a bad day, you exit the back door and come in the front again. Your dog will be there to do all over again!"

The last bundle of joy is still with us and may he be for many more years. Benson came to us only four weeks after Mindipin said goodbye. We had planned to wait and do some travel, but his Internet picture on a rescue site was too much to ignore. He, too, was a minpin, black and tan. He was only four months old. A breeder in Benson, Arizona, raised pups for pet stores but did not waste any money on those who had an illness or developed a problem that required surgery. Benson did and she spirited him away to a rescue group, People Assisting Kindred Spirits, Inc., [376] who subsequently posted his picture on the web. It was love at first sight and he was a tiny puppy. We drove to a Tanque Verde vet's office, where his foster mother worked, and were able to see this little guy. He raced all over the room and all we ever saw was a blur. He could not be adopted until the vet released him, following a minor surgery. The name Benson seemed appropriate because of the town from whence he came.

---

[375] https://rainbowsbridge.com/Poem.htm
[376] http://www.adoptapet.com/adoption_rescue/70756.html

Furthermore, dogs learn best to respond to their names generally if the chosen name is two syllables.[377]

Several days later, we drove to Desert Diamond Casino, [378] south of Tucson, where the group was showing rescue dogs. We met Donna, the rescue lady, and there was a tiny minpin in the cage. Everyone wanted him but we had already signed a contract, which was a rescue fee of $150. No deep discount here. We drove back to our house in SaddleBrooke and let him run freely in the yard. Much like Peppin, he had never been outside so it was a new experience with many new smells. He was not housebroken and cried all night for a few nights, until he got used to his new environment. I slept with him on my lap in an easy chair for a several nights, conditioning him even now to jump in my lap when he is uncertain or needy.

A few nights later, we had dinner guests. I wanted them to see Benson before we kenneled him for the remainder of the evening. So, as I was holding this frightened puppy, he graced with me with the same excretion my pet chicken had presented in Yoncalla. The white polo was never recoverable, indelibly marked with brown stuff, mostly glandular, that came out of Benson's fear of new experiences. Or was that Benson's rear?

He adjusted to life with us but was frightened out-of-doors. It took a while for him to walk on a leash. Now he eagerly walks three to four miles a day with us.

When Mindipin left us, we contracted for a Mexican cruise for ourselves as consolation, knowing we had no pet. In the meantime, Benson came into our lives. What would we do with him while on the cruise? We were to leave from San Diego, where we would leave our motor home, and be gone a week. Shirley located a sitter, Renee W., and we checked out her house. It seemed quite secure and she was a professional sitter, so she knew what to do. He was comfortable in her house and yard with other small dogs, so we had no worries.

We cruised to Ensenada, Puerto Vallarta and Manzanillo, enjoying our week. As soon as we returned, we drove to Renee's house to pick up Benson. He was fine and glad to see us. But her story was haunting.

The first day, all was fine. The second day, she went for groceries, leaving Benson in the house, which had a doggie door to the yard, with several other small dogs. When she returned, all the dogs were there

---

[377] http://www.ataboy.ca/puppy%20names.htm
[378] http://500nations.com/casinos/azDesertDiamondCasino.asp

except Benson. He was nowhere to be seen. He had scaled the four-foot fence, using his sharp nails to gain purchase on the wires, and disappeared over the other side.

Across the busy street was Balboa Park. She ran down the path into the park, eventually coming on a homeless gentleman on a bicycle with a large basket on the front. Benson was in the basket with a yellow rope around his neck. He was returned to Renee and carefully watched for the remainder of the week we were cruising. The story is daunting, if not miraculous. And we all have believed, ever since, that was not a homeless man. He was an angel. As Renee advised: "You have an extremely bright dog. His energy and motivation are very strong and he will always, always have to be watched carefully so as not to escape." How true her words have been proven.

Like all proud parents, we brag to ourselves how bright he is. It is not that we have to spell out words around him, but he knows by mood what is going on. If we have anxiety, he chirps. If we're relaxed, he sleeps. On Sunday afternoon, he knows it is typical to take him to the community Dog Park. He comes and looks languidly at Shirley to take him. If we use the term "dog park", he comes and paws at us. If it is 5 p.m. and he has not been fed, he comes and sits at my feet to remind me. If I use the word "golf cart", he runs and jumps into it the minute we're in the garage. We are told dogs learn all by operant and classical conditioning, [379] but there is no doubt in my mind our miniature pinscher can problem solve.

I can talk him into a poop when he is out in the yard, followed by encouraging him to pee. He seldom disappoints. Don't tell me this is operant conditioning.[380] He understands what I want and accomplishes it. Like all of us, Benson is willing to work for a reward, which is usually a little treat. The truth is simple: A miniature pinscher will do anything for food. Want them to sit? Provide a treat. Want them to heel? Provide a treat. Want them to conjugate French verbs? Provide a treat. It never fails.

Enough about dogs. They have been my greatest friends throughout my life, someone to talk to without receiving a judgmental response. Someone to watch trains with. Someone to provide company when alone. Someone who loves and forgives you, regardless of the sins you have committed that day, exactly like Christ does. And all good dogs go to heaven.[381] We can thank Pope Francis for that clarification.

---

[379] http://www.dogways.info/how-dogs-learn
[380] http://www.simplypsychology.org/operant-conditioning.html
[381] https://www.rt.com/news/214071-heaven-animals-pope-francis/

Among the numerous sayings about dogs, [382] these three are the best:

If there are no dogs in Heaven, then when I die I want to go where they went.

Will Rogers

Dogs' lives are too short. Their only fault, really.

Agnes Sligh Turnbull

Heaven's the place where all the dogs you've ever loved come to greet you.

Unknown

---

[382] http://thoughtcatalog.com/lorenzo-jensen-iii/2015/05/the-100-all-time-greatest-quotes-about-dogs/

Chapter 21   Let's Get Away From It All

Tucson is hot. When we first moved to Tucson in 1975, it began to cool down around the middle of September. In the spring, we never worried about 100-degree days again until Memorial Day. Whether global warming [383] is a reality, a political agenda or a myth, over the years, weather has changed. We now have a random hot spell in March and summer weather continues long into October. The question in Tucson has always been: "When will the ice break on the Santa Cruz," [384] which means, "When will we have our first 100-degree day?" A more telling fact, however, is how many consecutive days above 100-degrees occur each year. That number has increased annually, [385] but it is difficult to say whether it is global warming or a cycle. Whatever, Tucson is hot in the summer.

Transplanted Oregonians usually do not appreciate hot weather and that was true for Shirley and me. We always wanted to get away to a cooler region, as much as possible when one works through most of the summer as we did for 28 years. When we thought of Arizona, it was totally desert in our minds. But the Sonoran Desert is only one of the regions of the state. There are actually three: Colorado Plateau, the Central Highlands Transition Zone and the Basin and Range Province.[386]

Arizona is certainly not all desert, with the mean elevation at 4100 feet. There are mountainous areas, where you find pine, juniper and fir trees as well as aspen. We would escape to the high country each summer, sometimes a few days, sometimes a week or more, usually tied to Shirley's travels throughout the state as part of her Cooperative Extension duties.[387]

Although I usually taught one summer session, I was free for four or five weeks afterwards before Fall Semester began. Shirley would set county visitations so I could accompany her. A favorite place was Showlow, [388] Arizona, which is in Navajo County. There were a multitude of cabins for rent. With an elevation of over 6300 feet, it was much cooler than Tucson. Some of the cabins were rustic and full of dust bunnies, others, quite luxurious.

---

[383] http://www.ucsusa.org/global_warming#.VjNzsdD0jU4
[384] http://www.wrh.noaa.gov/twc/climate/Tucson100s/Tucson100s_1st100.php
[385] http://www.abc15.com/weather/heat-center/arizona-heat-facts
[386] http://www.ereferencedesk.com/resources/state-geography/arizona.html
[387] https://extension.arizona.edu
[388] https://en.wikipedia.org/wiki/Show_Low,_Arizona

One of my favorite photos is my sleeping on the bed, shortly after our arrival at a cabin, with Little Bit beside me. She was sleeping as if she, too, had just finished teaching summer classes. Our summer excursions would take us to all three Native American reservations. At the Hopi reservation, [389] we explored Walpi on First Mesa, Hotevilla on Third Mesa. We purchased a Kachina [390] and Hopi pots, all signed by native artists. Shirley was able to observe a Kachina dance emerge from a Kiva, thanks to a Native extension agent, who obtained special permission for a "white person" to observe these sacred rites. On the Navajo nation, [391] we visited Canyon de Chelly and Chinle, purchasing turquoise rings set in silver. Once we were invited to a Navajo house and shared an authentic meal with the family, which included fry bread and lamb. And we enjoyed a post-Christmas meal another time when Shirley's parents were visiting from Oregon with the extension agent, Grace R., at San Carlos, which is on the Apache reservation.

In our travels to Northern Arizona, we discovered the Mogollon Rim [392] as well as the towns of Pine-Strawberry, near Payson. We decided to purchase a small cabin as a second home in Pine in 1985. The cabin was only 1200 square feet, but it had an open great room with a fireplace, plus a bedroom suite on either end, each with a bathroom. There was a large deck, which we extended around the entire house. It was a wonderful retreat, so we used it both summer and winter. On Friday afternoons, we would leave the University at 4 p.m. and arrive in Pine four hours later. It was exactly 200 miles, door to door, and we never minded making the trip, if only overnight. No more dust bunny cabins. We had visitors to our cabin several times, including Rev. Joe and Jean B., as well as our parents. The neighbors were friendly and we had lots of social interaction.

Because our University salaries, particularly Shirley's, were growing, we needed some tax write-offs, that is, another mortgage so interest could be deducted. The Tax Reform Act of 1986 [393] changed the way one did business with the Federal Government. Formerly, all interest one paid on installment purchases, whether home, car or refrigerator, was deductible. With the reform, only interest on a primary and secondary home could be deducted. We had bit the bullet on the primary home in 1987 when we built a large house in Sabino Canyon, but more interest could be deducted on a second home as well.

---

[389] https://en.wikipedia.org/wiki/Hopi_Reservation
[390] http://www.native-languages.org/kachinas.htm
[391] http://www.navajo-nsn.gov/history.htm
[392] http://paysonrimcountry.com/Mountain-Recreation/Natural Landmarks/Mogollon-Rim
[393] http://legal-dictionary.thefreedictionary.com/Tax+Reform+Act+of+1986

We found a lot in the same development in Pine, Portal III, [394] and met with Steve I., local builder, to design a house. It turned out to be a barn, a nice one, but a barn. Three stories, two fireplaces, a basement, three bathrooms, each with a full bathroom, a loft and a two-car garage. It was perched on the side of a hill that mandated a driveway reminiscent of Bradford Street in San Francisco.[395]

It was a lovely house, but too big for a weekend get-a-way. The cozy cabin had given way to a palace. We enjoyed it for many weekends and vacations, but decided it could not be a retirement home because of its multi-levels.[396] We sold it to the lady whose granddaughter went out for a bite with Peppin. We purchased nine acres just outside the town and planned to move a travel trailer there. Eventually, we planned to build a small cabin, much like our first one, and have a weekend retreat once again.

Steve I., our former builder, had a great mind for investment. When we talked to him about a new cabin on the nine acres, he cautioned us not to rush. The land was valuable and would undoubtedly become more so in the future. He suggested subdivision. From my real estate license renewal classes, I knew there was a subdivision law in Arizona that allowed a parcel to be split into five lots without a public report.[397] We had the acreage surveyed and divided into five parcels with the intention of bringing in electricity, sewer and water. A gravel road was cut into the development and we constructed an RV garage on the lot we intended to keep. The others would eventually be sold.

Putting in electricity and cable was an easy task. It just cost a great deal of money. Sewer was another matter, but we eventually put in a small waste disposal plant that would service all five lots. Water was the toughest issue, which is not surprising in the desert Southwest. Our contractor put in a water line, but it was cut and deemed illegal by the local utility. The solution was to go before the Arizona Corporation Commission [398] and plead our case.

I represented us sans counsel and had to argue against the lawyer for

---

[394] http://portal3.org

[395] http://priceonomics.com/the-steepest-streets-in-/

[396] http://money.usnews.com/money/personal-finance/articles/2014/12/12/how-to-choose-the-perfect-retirement-home-for-you

[397] http://www.verdevalleyrealestate.com/Arizona_Subdivision_Laws/page_2234245.html

[398] http://www.azcc.gov

Robert H., CEO of Brooke Utilities. The legal profession has always held: "*In propria persona*", which means "anyone who represents himself in court has a fool for a client and an ass for an attorney." [399] I would never do it again, but with adequate documentation, we somehow prevailed. The Arizona Corporation Commission allowed a water meter for each lot, subject to signing onto a list and waiting our turn. Within two years, we were paying water bills on all five lots.

After ten years or more in the Pine area, we took a long look at what we might be doing in the next several years, which included retirement in less than a decade. We rented a Class C motor home through Cruise America and took it to the North Rim of Grand Canyon, [400] which is sheer magic compared to the South Rim. Peppin and Mindipin loved it. Shirley and Jim loved it, although I had trepidation about driving anything that big on the highway. Little did I realize then what a "big rig" really was.

Another time, we rented a Mobile Traveler from one of Shirley's colleagues, which also was a Class C coach. It was smaller and much older than our earlier rental but it got us there and back. We drove into Pagosa Springs [401] and Wolf Creek Pass [402] in Colorado. We discovered there was great freedom in motor homing.

Motor homes date from 1910 [403] and we were joining a group that traveled the country in a camping-car, as the French describe it. Drive to your destination and you have your own food, bed, clothes and whatever with you. We thought we would love it.

In 1996 we purchased our first Class A [404] motorhome, a 28-foot Bounder, T-28, manufactured by Fleetwood. It was a gas-puller, powered by a 460 HP Ford V-8 engine. We drove it for five years and never had a breakdown. It was comfortable, secure and relatively easy to maneuver and it towed our 1997 Honda CR-V.

Although we were still working at the UA, we managed to pull away for a month in summer to drive to Oregon. At Thanksgiving, we would travel to Laughlin, Nevada, to meet my brother, who also had a motor home. Christmas and Spring break were typically spent at the Chula Vista RV

---

[399] http://dictionary.law.com/default.aspx?selected=975
[400] http://www.grandcanyonlodgenorth.com
[401] https://en.wikipedia.org/wiki/Pagosa_Springs,_Colorado
[402] https://en.wikipedia.org/wiki/Wolf_Creek_Pass
[403] https://en.wikipedia.org/wiki/Motorhome
[404] https://en.wikipedia.org/wiki/List_of_recreational_vehicles

Resort and Marina, [405] south of San Diego. We knew then that life in an RV would be a big part of our retirement plans.

Always ready for the next, the bigger and the more expensive, I sprang for a diesel-pusher [406] in 2001, a 32-foot Country Coach Allure, powered by a Cummins 350 engine, coupled with a six-speed Allison transmission. This was true luxury but a whole different level of technology than a gas-puller. I would add, it was a whole different level of expense. Shirley loved the Bounder but gave me license to buy this big beast.

We had the silver-grey coach for almost four years and it was not the best of motorhomes. Nonetheless, it served us adequately although generating great anxiety on occasion. Its one slide was prone to open slightly while I was driving, which was nerve-wracking. It had a tendency to overheat in hot weather, since the radiator was in the back and the fans were not ample to cool the engine block sufficiently. It porpoised (a slang term used by RVers) on freeways, that is, the weight distribution was such that the backend was heavier, making the front-end bounce more than normal. Other than a hundred other small problems, the interior was beautifully crafted.

We retired from the UA in 2003, I in July, Shirley in September. We planned a retirement celebration at SaddleBrooke, the retirement community north of Tucson, to which we would be moving. One hundred seventy guests attended, including University and community friends. We catered the dinner but asked each guest to make a $25 donation to our endowment at the UA. By the time we retired, this fund, to which we had added over the years, was worth over $150,000. Since then, it has funded projects for faculty and students in the School of Music as well as the College of Agriculture and Life Sciences.

Soon after, we began our retirement schedule, which would be divided about half and half, six months in the coach on the road in summer and six months in SaddleBrooke in the winter.

A memorable experience happened in June 2004, as we were driving from Reno, Nevada toward I-5 in California in the Country Coach. It was a daylong trip. President Reagan had passed on June 5.[407] The state funeral was held at Washington National Cathedral on June 11, the day we were on the road. Since the television in the coach had an in-

---

[405] http://www.chulavistarv.com
[406] http://rv-roadtrips.thefuntimesguide.com/2009/12/pros_cons_rv_diesel_pusher.php
[407] https://en.wikipedia.org/wiki/Death_and_state_funeral_of_Ronald_Reagan

motion satellite dish, we watched the funeral while driving. Although this is not legal, for obvious reasons, I listened and Shirley watched from the passenger chair. We followed the funeral throughout the day and realized his casket was aboard Air Force One, headed for internment at the Ronald Reagan Presidential Library in Simi Valley, California, perhaps passing above us at some point in our journey. The President and we were both headed west toward the Pacific Ocean.

Our fascination with the Oregon Coast, which I rarely visited while growing up in Oregon, led to volunteer opportunities at lighthouses for five years. Heceta Head Lighthouse, [408] near Florence, Oregon was our first assignment. We received an RV site in Washbourne State Park and our work schedule was two days of four-hour shifts, twice a week. We conducted tours of the lighthouse, about ten to twelve visitors in a group, to the top of the lighthouse. Visitors would see the revolving first order Fresnel lens, [409] crafted in London before the lighthouse opened in 1893. Heceta's light could be seen twenty miles out to sea. We had to learn the history to become knowledgeable docents and answer the questions visitors asked.

Although we served two summers at Heceta, we also volunteered at Umpqua River Lighthouse [410] at Winchester Bay, Oregon. Heceta was part of the State Park system while Douglas County and the U.S. Coast Guard managed Umpqua. We spent four summers at this location. The volunteer group was much smaller and our motor home site was on Coast Guard property, on a high cliff overlooking the Pacific Ocean and the Umpqua River. We enjoyed the culture of Winchester Bay as well as Reedsport, a nearby town. While on that volunteer assignment, we provided piano/organ music for the Sunday services at the First Presbyterian Church.

The Umpqua Light, a first order Fresnel, which dates from the same time as Heceta, had a unique signature, two white flashes followed by a red, each 5 seconds apart. It's signal traveled 18 miles to sea. Each lighthouse throughout the world has a unique signal,[411] which aids in navigation along a coastline or shore of a lake. Mariners navigate with the List of Lights [412] for the bodies of water they are traversing. Rather than keeping a ship from crashing on the shoreline, a lighthouse's primary purpose is providing points of navigation for mariners. The advent of global positioning, however, has superannuated the purpose of

---

[408] https://en.wikipedia.org/wiki/Heceta_Head_Light
[409] http://science.howstuffworks.com/question244.htm
[410] https://en.wikipedia.org/wiki/Umpqua_River_Light
[411] https://www.marinersmuseum.org/sites/micro/cbhf/lighthouses/cbl003.html
[412] https://en.wikipedia.org/wiki/List_of_lights

lighthouses, at least for large ships. Local boaters, however, still depend on them.

One thing that was so advantageous about owning a Country Coach was RV service was available at the factory in Junction City, Oregon, near our summer locations. During our week of service, we would be moored in a lot close to the rail line that runs through town and hear the trains all night long, probably eight each night. And they sounded their whistle six times as they rolled through town, once for each of the six crossings. That's a lot of whistles but those trains were all going somewhere and going fast. But I generally slept through most of those whistles, having lived so near the train tracks in Mosier.

We also attended the annual RV rallies, either at Eugene or Albany. We could use our off-days at the lighthouses to attend these rallies. There would be classes on maintaining your coach, including engine, tranny and tire service. Every evening, there were cocktail parties and dinners, with first class entertainment. The company, alas, was spending itself into bankruptcy. Country Coach went out of business in 2008.

In 2005, after several problems with our 32-foot coach, we purchased a 2006 37-foot Allure. It had a Cummins 400 ISL engine, [413] which is an efficient engine used in many freight trucks, as well as four slide-outs. Although the new coach was bigger, it delivered better mileage and better torque, even with the larger engine. This was a unique coach because it had a tag axle, which made turning into tight areas easier as well as providing a heavier footprint with eight wheels on the pavement when driving. The 2006 Allure was used for our annual trek to Oregon to work the lighthouses as well as Christmas treks to Chula Vista or Las Vegas.

In the summer of 2008, when Benson was still new to our family, we took an assignment in Michigan at Forty-mile Point Lighthouse, [414] near Alpena and Rogers City. The RV trip to Michigan was ambitious in a motor home, taking ten days so we could stay a few days in some locations. We traveled from Tucson to New Mexico, across the panhandle of Texas, and then up Tornado Alley, [415] Oklahoma City, Tulsa, Branson, St. Louis and through Chicago. We followed the weather on the in-motion television as we drove, always trying to be aware of which county we were in and which county was having turbulent weather. We never hit a tornado, but the day we passed through Tulsa, one had occurred the night before. Trees and power lines were down throughout the area.

---

[413] http://cumminsengines.com/uploads/docs/4971107.pdf
[414] http://www.40milepointlighthouse.org
[415] https://en.wikipedia.org/wiki/Tornado_Alley

Forty-mile Point Lighthouse was a small lake light, with a fourth-order Fresnel. Its range was ten miles. There were few visitors to this region, at least during our tenure, which was two weeks. We did tours and managed the gift shop. We also enjoyed visiting other lighthouses in the region. Surprisingly, Michigan has more lighthouses than any other state, over 120 in working condition, but there were as many as 247 functional lighthouses in past years.[416] Michigan has more shoreline than any other state, because portions of Lake Michigan, Superior and Huron border it. In the heyday of ore shipping into the smelters of Chicago and Detroit, ship traffic was heavy and lighthouses were essential for secure transit.

Our Country Coach performed wonderfully on this trip. When our two-week assignment was finished, we headed west, stopping in Door County, Wisconsin to visit friends who live in SaddleBrooke, our retirement community in Tucson. We also stopped in Minnesota to visit another couple. We always joked with both couples that we drove over 5000 miles to have dinner, whereas we could have simply walked a few blocks to do the same thing in SaddleBrooke.

This extensive trip took us across Wisconsin, Minnesota, North Dakota and all of Montana. We finally landed in Coeur d'Alene, Idaho, where there was a series of bike trails, including the Centennial Trail [417] and Trail of the Coeur d'Alene's.[418] The former runs from Higgins Point near the lake to Spokane; the latter is a paved-over rail line for 72 miles.

Since we had not used our bikes much in Michigan, we tried out Idaho trails, each going his or her separate way. As it turned out, one afternoon we met in front of Riverfront Lofts and Condos on the Spokane River. I wanted to take a look and Shirley reluctantly came along. This development had riverfront condos on one side of the building with a city view on the opposite.

Of course, we bought one. It made no sense and never did, but we purchased a corner unit that had been intended for the architect, Eric H., that had an incredible view of the river and the U.S. Highway 95 bridge crossing the river. Condo prices were high and only seven units of the 42 had actually sold.

We took the coach to Reedsport to fulfill our docent duties at Umpqua for the summer, but returned to Coeur d'Alene in September to furnish the unit. Again, it made no sense, since we already had a rolling second

---

[416] http://www.chsd.us/~pjdurbin/lighthouses_of_michigan2.htm
[417] http://www.traillink.com/trail/north-idaho-centennial-trail.aspx
[418] http://friendsofcdatrails.org/CdA_Trail/#.VjYqD9D0jU4

home with the Country Coach. But we did it nonetheless; choosing some nice Stressless recliners and a Natuzzi sofa, plus upscale washer and dryer. What fun it was to spend the money to feather the Idaho nest.

We enjoyed this condo for seven years, returning in the summer to spend part of our time there. But we also traveled in the motor home to the Oregon coast, where we owned an RV lot at Pacific Shores Motor Coach Resort in Newport as well as Las Vegas, where we owned another lot at Las Vegas Motor Coach Resort. Time to lighten up and decide whether we wanted a motor home or a condo. Quite an adventure!

There were particular joys in Coeur d'Alene. It is a beautiful city and everything needed is close, no more than ten minutes away. The Resort area, where we frequently had dinner, was stellar. The downtown park always seemed to have an event. While there, we volunteered twice for the Coeur d'Alene Ironman,[419] which is held in late June. We also enjoyed church services at Lake City Community Church.[420] But most of all, we enjoyed the biking trails. With a bike trail almost at our front door, I did bike rides several times a week, if not to Higgins Point, eleven miles east, then west to state line, where Idaho meets Washington.

The Trail of the Coeur d'Alene's was always a rewarding outing. We would take the bikes on the car to Wallace, Cataldo, Rose Lake or Plummer, ride out ten miles and back. Over our time in Idaho, we probably did the entire 72 miles, two or three times, in installments, of course. Once, we encountered and saw a bull moose in rut, just a few feet off the trail, which required one to pedal very fast to avoid confrontation. Other times, bear scat was seen. The "Rails to Trails" program, jointly funded by the mining companies and the Federal government, allowed bikers to really see the interior back woods of Northern Idaho. In addition, it cleaned up a great deal of mining pollution.

We even drove up to the condo some winters, spending time over Christmas to enjoy cold weather and snow. The first winter we had 84 inches of snow. The drive from Tucson to Coeur d'Alene is 1500 miles, which required three nights in a motel, but we made the winter trip at least three or four times. We even navigated ice on the last trip, traveling 30 mph over treacherous roads for hundreds of miles. That is probably one reason we decided to sell the condo in 2015. In addition, we were moving back and forth from the Country Coach to the condo as we

---

[419] http://www.ironman.com/triathlon/events/americas/ironman/coeur-dalene/athletes/course.aspx#axzz3qHptPbqX
[420] http://lakecitycc.org/when-and-where/

performed at festivals, a major swap of clothes, appliances, food and emotions each time. It became a weary exercise.

There is one other reason we decided to part with the condo. In summer of 2014, after servicing our 2006 Allure, we stopped by Premier RV in Junction City to buy a sewer hose. We came out with a different motor home, a 2006 Country Coach Intrigue. There was no particular reason that we wanted a different motor home, but when we looked at this 40-foot model, it all clicked. And it has been a good coach, minor repairs here and there, but nothing untypical of any motor home. I also realized, with this coach, what "big rig" really means when discussing and driving RVs.

Our theme in retirement has been *Let's Get Away From It All*, best summarized in Frank Sinatra's compelling rendition of the song of the same name. This has become our theme song:

Let's take a boat to Bermuda
Let's take a plane to Saint Paul.
Let's take a kayak to Quincy or Nyack,
Let's get away from it all.

Let's take a trip in a trailer,
No need to come back at all.
Let's take a powder to Boston for chowder,
Let's get away from it all.[421]

---

[421] http://www.azlyrics.com/lyrics/franksinatra/letsgetawayfromitall.html

Chapter 22   Socializing in Social Security City

Since we retired, we have spent five or six months in the motor home or condo away from Tucson. What about the other half of year? This was spent in Tucson.

Our house in Sabino Canyon, in which we had lived for 17 years, was not a good place to retire. It was in need of remodeling and showed its age. It was also too big. Most of the current homeowners, who had bought out the first wave of owners in the development, were professionals with jobs that took them to the city daily, if not on travel around the country. We would wave as they drove by, whether they were taking children to or from school in their Mercedes or BMWs, as we were walking Peppin and Mindipin. The houses that we had all built in the 1980s had appreciated so much that only high-level professionals could afford them. We were one of the few original owners in our community.

For us, it was time for a senior ghetto, that is, an age-restricted community, 55 and older.   Shirley did due diligence on this one, knowing we needed a change after retirement.   SaddleBrooke,[422] a Robson development northwest of Tucson became the community of choice.   We made several visits to the development, which is a golf community, and choose a lot as well as a model to be built. Lots were small, prices big and restrictions severe, but we managed to fund and construct a 2600 sq. ft. house in one of the units three years before we actually retired. We furnished it very sparsely so we would come out on weekends and pretend we were retired. It was a comfortable feeling and a goal to be achieved in the near future.

Soon after we retired in 2003, we took an autumn trip to Oregon, returning late in the year. The annual variety show of SaddleBrooke, which had been staged every other year since the dawn of time, was in rehearsals. I wanted nothing to do with it but Shirley went to participate in the chorus. The director suggested I come and reinforce the musical ensemble with my synthesizer, which I agreed to try. It was quite apparent the musical and stage directors were not getting along. At one point, I was asked to accompany the group on the piano while the musical director led the chorus. That started it all.

We went home after the rehearsal and there was a phone call. "Would Jim like to be the musical director?" Apparently, after we left, the tension had exploded and the musical director stormed out, leaving the show. It was not exactly the way I wanted to use my skills in a new community, but I agreed. We rehearsed for the next month or so with a

---

[422] http://www.saddlebrooke.org

cast of 30 and performed three nights in the SaddleBrooke Mountain View ballroom in March 2004.

The variety show script was amateurish, with hackneyed jokes that had gone out with vaudeville and musical numbers that never should have been staged, at least in a public arena that required the audience to buy a ticket. Shirley and I decided we could write a better script and mounted a production the following spring, which we dubbed: *SaddleBrooke Send-Up: A Satirical Sensation.* It would be a satire on "active adult living" in a retirement community.

And lampoon we did. We took well-known songs of the 1940's and 1950's and set them to new lyrics, a centuries old musical procedure called "contrafactum".[423] (Another term is "parody".) In the Middle Ages, church leaders used popular street songs and set them to Latin words in order to attract commoners into churches. During the Protestant Reformation,[424] the opposite occurred. Catholic tunes were set in the vernacular, the local language, so worshippers could sing in their daily speech. More recently, contrafactum has been used as a satirical device.

Shirley and I would select a song. One would provide the first draft of new lyrics, the second would edit. And then, back and forth, until it had the comic punch we wanted and the words fit the musical score.

To lampoon the quality of construction of our new community, we provided these words to the tune of *This Old House*:

Verse One

This old house has cost me plenty,
This old house has cost a lot,
This old house has been positioned
On a very tiny plot.
This old house was framed quite quickly,
This old house was roofed and sealed,
Now it leaks in all the monsoons,
And the paint's begun to peel.

Chorus

We can play our tennis matches,
We can golf as oft we will,
We can use the fitness center,

---

[423] http://www.southampton.ac.uk/~wpwt/notes/contraf.htm
[424] http://www.theopedia.com/protestant-reformation

Where we tread upon the mill.
We can meet at happy hour
And drink bourbon, beer and wine,
Then we drive our little golf-carts
Madly home so we can dine.

Verse Two

This old house was insulated,
This old house has R-16,
This old house is quite expensive
To condition, cool and clean.
This old house is not a track home,
But this house is not unique,
I can see its cloned examples,
As I travel down the street.

Verse Three

This old house is now surrounded
By a hundred houses, more!
I can hear my noisy neighbors
Every time I use the door.
This old house still has a mortgage,
This old house is not debt free,
Twice a year I pay much money
For the high homeowners' fee. [425]

The show was a success. We sold out every night to a capacity crowd. SaddleBrooke residents loved to laugh at themselves. In addition, we had accumulated a group of local thespians, which loved to be on the boards, entertaining audiences and making them laugh. We had actors, singers and dancers. It was time to create a club for these shows and that came in an organization called S.P.A.G. (SaddleBrooke Performing Arts Group). [426] An organizational meeting was held and over 60 SaddleBrooke residents joined the theatre group. Almost immediately, the group was granted official club status by charter within the SaddleBrooke Homeowners Association as well as a 501(c)(3), a tax-exempt nonprofit organization, [427] by the I.R.S. [428]

---

[425] O'Brien, James and Shirley. SaddleBrooke Send-Up: A Satirical Sensation, 2005.
[426] SaddleBrooke Performing Arts Guild
[427] https://en.wikipedia.org/wiki/501(c)_organization
[428] https://www.irs.gov/Charities-&-Non-Profits/Charitable-Organizations/Exemption-Requirements-Section-501(c)(3)-Organizations

Two years later, 2007, we performed a sequel in the new Desert View Performing Arts Center, [429] the community theater, which opened earlier in the year. We programmed four nights and sold out four nights, seating over 400 at each show.

Again, we used well-known songs to lampoon something about the community. It hit the right note with our patrons and we were on to producing more shows. It had been suggested that dinner theatre would be a nice addition for the community. The rental fee for the local theatre was prohibitive, and rehearsal space was limited so we decided to try our luck with a Christmas dinner theatre. *Christmas in the Brooke* was born, and ran for four seasons. The songs were familiar but with new lyrics. Three-courses were paraded and served, each time with the cast moving about the ballroom singing these words from *Food, Glorious Food* from *Oliver.*[430]

Food, Glorious Food"
Our Christmas tradition,
Food, Glorious Food"
From SaddleBrooke kitchen,
This holiday food we bring,
Your palate will savor,
Side dishes and vegetables,
Full of flavor.

Food, Glorious food.
You're anxious to try it.
Three courses are good,
To throw off your diet.
Chef Robert has done his best,
His SaddleBrooke gift, Oh!
Food, wonderful food,
Marvelous food,
Glorious food.

---

[429] http://saddlebrooketwo.com/desertview_main1.htm
[430] https://en.wikipedia.org/wiki/Oliver!

A particular favorite was an original paraphrase of Clement Clarke Moore's *T'was the Night Before Christmas*.[431] Our version was SaddleBrooke-specific:

'T'was the night before Christmas in SaddleBrooke fair,
Not a creature was stirring, like ev'ry night there.
The golfers had gone, the fairways were bare
In hopes all the divots would get some repair.

The tennis courts empty, the craft room abandoned
The programs on TV appeared to be random.
And I in my bathrobe and Ma in her turban
Were sipping our eggnogs spiked freely with bourbon.

When out on the gravel there arose such a noise
I sprang from the sofa without any poise.
Away to the window I flew like a missile
Tore open the shutters and gave a loud whistle.

The moon on the crest of the newly mowed green
Showed a vision from my backyard that seemed like a dream.
When what to my wondering eyes could be seen?
But a hopped-up old cart golf completely in green.

With a little old driver decked out in bright red,
He should have been home tucked tight in his bed.
More rapid than Harleys, his golf cart it flew,
While he coughed and he wheezed and expelled an "a choo".

As mesquite growth before the monsoon blows round,
As it spins and careens and then falls to the ground,
So up to the fourth green the golf cart did go,
With the geezer maneuvering it both to and fro

And then, in a twinkling, I saw on the course,
He was driving a golf ball with no great remorse.
As I drew in my head and was ready to scream,
He slammed the ball hard and it plopped on the green.

He was dressed in Bermudas, with a jaunty red cap
And a red polo shirt that he'd bought at The Gap.

---

[431] http://www.nightbeforechristmas.biz/poem.htm

A bundle of clubs he had thrown in his cart.
The beer he had probably bought at the Mart.

His gait was unsteady since he suffered no thirst
The brew he was chugging was more than his first.
He moved on the green as performing a dance.
While the belt that he wore stretched tight round his pants.

The stump of a stogie he clamped in his teeth
As the smell of it drifted ov'r us without relief.
He had a round belly and round ruddy face
One you'd expect from a SaddleBrooke ace.

His drive was appalling, his putting far worse
He exceeded par with an audible curse.
As he finished ten strokes, he left in disgust
Walking back to his cart, he uttered a cuss.

Then, he sprang to his cart, racing to the next tee.
He played after dark to escape the green fee.
But I heard him exclaim as he vanished from sight,
"You can save lots of dough if you just golf at night." [432]

We then extended the success of these shows to a version called *Romance in the Brooke*, lampooning "senior" love, with all of the complications of second and third marriages, infidelity, wills and trusts, divorce and plastic surgery to stay eternally young. *Someone To Watch Over Me* [433] became a plea to re-do what nature had allowed to age:

There's a somebody I'm longing to see,

I hope that he turns out to be,

Someone who can re-make me.

I've some blemishes that need to be lost,

Botox the sags, regardless the cost,

To one who can re-make me.

---

[432] O'Brien, James and Shirley, Christmas in the Brooke, 2008.
[433] https://en.wikipedia.org/wiki/Someone_to_Watch_Over_Me_(song)

I know that he will be the surgeon
To make me look brand new,
To my looks he carries the key.

Won't you tell him please to pull up my bust,
Tush re-adjust, he has my trust.
Someone who can re-make me.

There were ten shows in ten years, all running several nights. All the shows were successful but there were reasons not to continue. It was difficult to work with the culinary staff at SaddleBrooke's two Homeowners Associations to provide a gourmet meal that was affordable. Rehearsal space was limited, even when available for booking. Dealing with a diverse audience was difficult, since seniors can be demanding in their tastes and rights. Our cast, too, had multiple interests and could not always commit to a rehearsal schedule that would deliver quality. In 2011, we decided it was time for someone to take over. Shirley and I were tired, since the entire enterprise depended on us to write, direct, market, rehearse, negotiate and perform. It became a year-round job that took most of our time, whether in Tucson or not. No one did take our place and we still have pleas for us to write another script, mount another show and put our friends on stage.

S.P.A.G. had accumulated large pots of money from these shows, even after expenses were paid. The group funded an endowment at the University of Arizona's School of Theatre, Film and Television [434] for worthy students majoring in musical theatre who needed a boost their last year in school to start their professional career. This alliance was good for S.P.A.G. and the School, with reciprocal exchanges for performances and receptions. The endowment now exists in perpetuity.

In addition to our career as theatrical entrepreneurs in retirement, Shirley and I participated in other activities in SaddleBrooke, including Cycle Masters, [435] the biking club, and SaddleBrooke Pickleball Association. [436] I also took numerous classes in Spanish and accomplished hikes with the local club. Senior living, like all units with

---

[434] www.tftv.arizona.ed
[435] http://saddlebrookecyclemasters.org
[436] http://spa.clubexpress.com

which one affiliates, creates likes and dislikes. Fortunately, the former outweigh the latter. One finds there are numerous friends and acquaintances that will assist you in just about any endeavor. There are many rules that limit what and when you can do certain things, but they preserve the integrity of the community, which helps maintain home values.

In the middle of one of these shows, for some unknown reason, we decided to buy another house in the community. The first house we built in SaddleBrooke in 2001 proved to be wrong for us. It had too many small rooms and sat on too small a lot. One Sunday afternoon in 2007, we biked to the new section, the Preserve, [437] and found a spec house. It was love at first sight and we bought it. It was not bigger, but had an open floor plan and a large backyard, with an awesome view. It is still home. And there is no rail track outside coaxing me to move somewhere else. This may be it.

---

[437] http://www.robson.com/communities/the-preserve

Chapter 23   Can't Spend It All

One should not design his or her life to be rich, whatever that means. No one even seems to agree what wealth means.[438] Is it income? Is it savings? Is it retirement accounts or the value of your home? The answer to this riddle is another riddle. Shirley and I are comfortable. And we were throughout our careers, even though we had mortgages and car payments. We do not have these encumbrances in retirement. We carry no debt, not even on the one credit card, which is paid off monthly.

How is wealth accumulated? Much like the question of wealth, there is no easy answer but three points seem to assist one to work towards wealth.[439] You need to earn it, save it and invest it. Those three things we certainly did.

When we returned from Australia and moved to Tucson in 1975, we had a reasonable pot of money from the income tax refund we received when leaving the country. That was a starting point.

In addition, we had a home in Oregon, not paid for, but which had doubled in value in the two years we had been out of the country. It sold within our first year in Arizona. In Tucson, we purchased a nice townhome with very little down, knowing the interest on the mortgage was deductible on taxes. In addition, we took some of the Australian tax money and bought a 3.3-acre parcel of vacant land on the far eastside, thinking we might build on it.

As our salaries increased, which was never dramatically, I kept looking for land opportunities and within five years we owned 40 acres on the northwest side, 20 acres near Ryan field, 20 acres in Avra Valley plus the 3.3 acres on the eastside. With Tucson's growth, particularly with the arrival of IBM [440] in 1977-78, land was needed for houses. Before tax reform, all the interest on these loans was deductible. We had invested a great deal of the Australian tax refund in tax-exempt municipal bonds. When payments came due, I clipped the coupons and made the payments.

In addition, Shirley's parents, Al and Lydia were generous in their gifts to us. They were downsizing their estate and gave the maximum allowed by law to us for several years. This was subsequently invested in more real estate. They did chide me for "not having fun with the money", but I

---

[438] http://www.financialsamurai.com/how-much-income-do-you-consider-to-be-rich/
[439] http://www.investopedia.com/articles/pf/07/three_steps.asp
[440] https://www-03.ibm.com/ibm/history/exhibits/tucson/tucson_initial.html

assured them, in time, we would have a good time. And that has proven to be correct.

The little townhouse was sold for a bit of a profit and we built another home in Hidden Valley. After ten years in that house, we sold it for double what we paid. The Federal government is quite benevolent in allowing a couple to forego capital gains when their house has appreciated less than $500,000.[441] We took advantage of that two additional times in the next several years, which means the profit is not subject to tax, unless you do it within two years of purchase. We had not.

In the days that houses were increasing in value beyond expectation, it paid to move up, move up and move up. When we finally sold our last house in Sabino Canyon, we walked away with a pot of cash that made the Australian largesse look like tip money. This scenario, alas, has changed since 2008, when the housing bubble finally burst and owners began to realize a house was not an ATM.

Housing and land were very profitable for us. The 3.3 acres was a special example of appreciation. Richard H., a local realtor who also ran for Congress a few years later, told us when we purchased from him: "Don't ever get sentimental over a piece of real estate. It is only a commodity to buy and sell." This advice has proven correct. When we bargained to sell the 3.3 acres, it had appreciated ten-fold from what we had paid. The Avra Valley land, which we split and sold on installment, similarly appreciated ten-fold. That is how wealth is built.

When Shirley and I were married, I asked her if she would explore "budgeting" with me. We would pool our money. She would have her allowance and I would have mine. But all the other needs for living would come from our combined salaries. She was willing. Consequently, we learned to live within a budget for 43 years of our marriage. There is nothing like accrual accounting [442] to allocate revenue and expenses and be certain they are equal. My sister used this concept early in her adult life. When she received a paycheck, she would put a set amount of cash in jars, one for car insurance, another for medical, yet another for clothes. When expenses came in, she retrieved the cash amount from the appropriate jar to pay the bill. Accrual accounting works the same way sans the jars.

---

[441] http://www.bankrate.com/finance/money-guides/home-sale-capital-gains-1.aspx
[442] http://www.entrepreneur.com/encyclopedia/accrual-accounting

With our combined earnings, we found we could live on one and a half salaries, not two. The difference went into a tax-sheltered account, [443] which also reduced our federal and state tax obligations. Eventually that money has to be withdrawn at age 70 ½, but that seemed a long time away in our mid-careers. It has come to pass, however. The Feds do want their tax dollars eventually.

Admittedly, we lived on the cheap and still do. It was actually fun to figure out ways to save money without denying ourselves. We drove cars for eight to ten years, did not eat out much, entertained at home, bought clothes on sale or at thrift shops. Our vacations were always tied to Shirley's job, that is, traveling to a conference and having part of the meals and lodging covered by per diem. The only problem with this mentality is that now, it is hard to break that mold and spend the money, when there is no need to save for the future.

We also invested in a cabin in northern Arizona, at Pine-Strawberry, eventually selling the first cabin for a profit, the second cabin as well and then developing nine acres of vacant land we owned into a subdivision. This story of wealth building was unbelievable, even to us who had planned the investment from the day we purchased it.

We never dreamed that splitting the nine acres of prime forestland and then putting in water, sewer, electricity and cable would result in mind-boggling profit. The project was accomplished debt-free and we realized we had five lots, each about one and a half acres to place on the market. We contacted Windermere Real Estate and negotiated a contract for them to represent us as sellers' agents. Butch J. was the broker and he asked what we would like to receive for each lot. I knew what we had invested in each and wanted to make a $10,000 profit for each. I set the price and Butch said: "Let's double what you want!" I argued, but this wise realtor said we should at least try. Within two weeks, everything had been sold, cash on the line, at Butch's price. Capital gains were very steep for us in 2005!

The other perk we had at the University of Arizona was defined-benefit retirement systems. Mine was the Arizona State Retirement System, [444] Shirley's, Federal Employees Retirement System.[445] With my extra online courses the last three years of teaching, I pumped up my retirement annuity to be greater than my normal salary. Shirley's was equally generous. And we both qualified for Social Security benefits. The extra salary again elevated this entitlement. In addition, I had paid into

---

[443] http://www.investopedia.com/terms/t/taxshelter.asp
[444] https://www.azasrs.gov/content/retirement-central
[445] https://www.opm.gov/retirement-services/fers-information/

F.I.C.A. for over 50 years, starting at the packinghouse job where I repaired lug boxes at age 14. The University of Arizona was also generous in paying all unused sick leave we had accumulated over the years, which was another pocket of cash.

What do you do with this wealth when it suddenly is in your bank account? You give some of it away. The Lord provides it all to begin with and the Holy Bible gives instruction on giving back. Hebrew scriptures mandate 10% [446] whereas Christian scriptures do not specify, except the church usually mandates: "Whatever you give, give cheerfully". Shirley and I always felt 10% was a good deal compared to Islam, where the faithful are admonished to give 2 ½ % of their wealth (about 1/40th) annually.[447] Zakat is considered a tax to Moslems. Tithing is not and seems a bargain compared to that specific pillar of Islam. We presently give 15-20% annually, not just to the church we attend, but to charities as well as medical and educational endowments. You can't take it with you and as our minister portrayed vividly a few Sundays ago: "Did you ever see a U-Haul behind a hearse?" [448]

The key to financial success and security is really spending less than you make and saving the rest wisely. It was never hard to do, beginning with Mom's requirement that I split the $15 of cherry money to provide needs, wants and savings. After 13 years of retirement, we still budget, we use accrual accounting and we save.

---

[446] http://www.gotquestions.org/tithing-Christian.html
[447] https://en.wikipedia.org/wiki/Zakat
[448] attributed to Moore, James W. Have You Ever Seen a Hearse Pulling a Trailer?, 2009

Chapter 24   Then, Now and To Be

Mike R., pastor at Lake City Community Church in Coeur d'Alene delivers memorable sermons with staying power. The one I particularly remember was an hourglass analogy. He drew a picture of an hourglass, showed the sand flowing from top to bottom and said our lives were much like this. We can see how much sand is on the bottom, but we do not know how much longer the sand will keep falling from the top. There is nothing we can do about what is already fallen, but we can maximize our lives while sand is still falling.

What is life expectancy? [449] It's as long as you live. And for most of us, it is never enough. Do we determine how long we live or does a healthy or unhealthy lifestyle make any difference?   The Scriptural interpretation is well documented in the Holy Bible.[450] Nutritionists and medical gurus, however, claim we can extend our life by exercising, eating the right foods and obtaining the necessary amount of sleep each night.[451]   Perhaps our days are predestined and the healthy lifestyle simply gives us better quality of life until we die. I have no idea.

I have lived over three-quarters of a century and yet feel that I can live a while longer. But one's body does change through the years, which means we age. Mitosis, the process whereby a cell divides to create two new cells, was discovered in the late 1800's,[452] so we are aware that many of our cells are continually being replaced with new ones. Does each generation of new cells result in an exact replication? Perhaps, yes, perhaps, not, and certainly not forever.

When we take a document and photocopy it on a printer, the resolution is never as good as the original. If each subsequent photocopy is then copied, over time, whatever is on the sheet becomes little more than a series of dots.

Similarly, there is a musical composition by Alvin Lucier titled *I Am Sitting in a Room*, [453] which is a metaphor of this process and perhaps of how the cells of our bodies change over time. In the 1969 recording, he recites several phrases into a tape recorder. Once the recording was made, it was played back and re-recorded. This re-recording was then

---

[449] http://www.news-medical.net/health/Calculating-Life-Expectancy.aspx
[450] http://www.openbible.info/topics/days_are_numbered
[451] https://www.fightaging.org/introduction/
[452] https://en.wikipedia.org/wiki/Mitosis
[453] https://en.wikipedia.org/wiki/I_Am_Sitting_in_a_Room

recorded again and again several times, creating a new generation of the original phrases each time. After 47 repetitions, Lucier's original text was no longer discernible. It had totally mutated into something else, almost a series of grunts and groans, much like the photocopy, which will eventually become a series of dots and blank spaces.

Perhaps this is what happens with our bodies as we age. The cells duplicate themselves but over time, never exactly. Eventually they mutate into something different from what they originally were. No amount of egg whites, kale, exercise, fillers and lifts will make us what we once were.

The moral of the story is we age and then we die. The longer we are alive, the more sand is in the bottom of the hourglass and the less on top. But for now, I'm still here and I'm still writing. It would be bizarre to remain forever young, as Dorian Gray [454] did. He sold his soul and lived a libertine life, while his ageing was reflected only in his portrait, that is, until the very end. So it is "better to be over the hill than under it". [455]

Shirley and I enjoyed remarkably good health throughout our adult life. There were rare sick days. I had a few hernia repairs, but we had our annual wellness exams and seemed destined to be sound for years. However, after a series of questionable blood tests, in 2012 Shirley was advised to see a hematologist. He recommended a bone marrow biopsy [456] and the results showed she had MDS (myelodysplastic syndromes), [457] which is a type of bone marrow cancer.

The only cure for MDS is a bone marrow transplant, [458] which works successfully for some, particularly for younger patients. We choose not to go that route, but, rather, try chemotherapy. Chemo for MDS is a hypermethylating agent, [459] which means treatment with Dacogen (decitabine) or Vidaza (azacitidine). Shirley took Dacogen for five months, five infusions in her surgically implanted port catheter once a month. There were additional biopsies to test if the drug were working and it was.

---

[454] https://en.wikipedia.org/wiki/The_Picture_of_Dorian_Gray
[455] https://www.pinterest.com/annette2546/better-over-the-hill-than-under-it/
[456] https://www.nlm.nih.gov/medlineplus/ency/article/003934.htm
[457] https://bethematch.org/for-patients-and-families/learning-about-your-disease/myelodysplastic-syndromes/
[458] http://www.seattlecca.org/diseases/bone-marrow-transplant-facts.cfm
[459] http://www.cancer.org/cancer/myelodysplasticsyndrome/detailedguide/myelodysplastic-syndromes-treating-chemotherapy

In Coeur d'Alene, Dr. K., an oncologist, announced the disease was in remission and she remained off chemo for seven months. Upon return to Tucson in the fall, Dr. T. put her back on chemo, this time on Vidaza, which has a longer track record, at least according to the research journals. We had visited the Moffitt Cancer Center and Research Institute[460] in Tampa earlier. Dr. L., world-authority on treatment of MDS, recommended the switch to Vidaza. This required seven infusions per month, one and a half weeks for treatment in each cycle. This regimen was followed until May 2015, when the chemo began to fail. Her three bloodlines, white cells, red cells and platelets did not recover between chemo treatments.

There were visits to the Taussig Cancer Institute [461] at the Cleveland Clinic to confer with Dr. S., who said stay on the Vidaza. There was a trip to the Fred Hutchinson Cancer Research Center in Seattle to confer with Dr. S. There was no magic in any of these places, only affirmation that Vidaza should be taken until it fails.

And when it fails, and it did, there are few options. Without treatment, MDS progresses to AML (Acute Myeloid Leukemia).[462] There was another trip to Seattle where Dr. S. prescribed Promacta (eltrombopag),[463] which might boost platelet production in the blood. The price of years of chemo is a reduction in the production of white and red blood cells as well as platelets. Immunity sinks to level zero and Shirley was continually at risk for infection.

We felt there was always hope, but it depended on finding a clinical trial or a miraculous cure. Research [464] continues daily on MDS and leukemia and we were hoping some young assistant professor at a teaching hospital, with an M.D. and a Ph.D., would earn his or her tenure by making a remarkable discovery that would positively affect all patients. It would take a giant of a gene-jockey.

These have been and are trying times for the three of us, Shirley, Benson and me. He reflects our moods. He also reduces our stress by making us laugh and requiring two, if not three, walks a day, which elevates

---

[460] https://moffitt.org
[461] http://my.clevelandclinic.org/ccf/media/files/outcomes/2013/outcomes-cancer.pdf
[462] http://www.cancer.org/cancer/leukemia-acutemyeloidaml/
[463] http://www.drugs.com/promacta.html
[464] http://www.cancer.org/cancer/myelodysplasticsyndrome/detailedguide/myelodysplastic-syndromes-new-research

everyone's spirits. The future was uncertain and living one day at a time became a necessity, not a cliché.[465]

When we returned from our 2015 summer in Oregon, we met with Dr. R. [466] at The University of Arizona Cancer Center. He encouraged us to seek a clinical trail. Through a telephone conference with the Aplastic Anemia & MDS International Foundation, [467] where we had funded a research grant, in Washington, D.C., we were advised to consult with Dr. Courtney DiNardo [468] at the MD Anderson Cancer Center [469] in Houston, Texas.

We flew out for an initial consultation in November 2015 and were told to return as soon as possible, since Shirley was eligible for a clinical trial, using AG-120, [470] an oral therapy developed by Agios, [471] a biopharmaceutical company in Cambridge, Massachusetts. We returned to Houston in our motor home soon after in early December, covering 1100 miles in four days, Honda CR-V in tow. Shirley underwent interviews, tests, blood draws, EKGs and bone marrow biopsies and was admitted to the program. As I write, some two weeks into this clinical trial, which is in Phase Two, she is experiencing response to AG-120, which means her blood values are moving upward towards a normal range. The drug appears to be working and we praise the Lord, as well as the army of family and friends who have prayed for its success. This was the next step and we were in the right place, at the right time, with the right clinical trial, with the right doctor and at the right medical institution.

All of my life, "cancer" was the dreaded "C" word, practically a death sentence when anyone was so diagnosed. As a child, I remember its victims usually had surgery or radiation, but few survived. Gradually, chemotherapy was integrated into the menu of options for treatment. Nonetheless, all three therapies were generic to cancer, not to a specific cancer. Thus, chemotherapy may kill the cancerous cells but it kills normal cells as well. That is why some patients lose their hair.

---

[465] https://www.psychologytoday.com/blog/the-happiness-project/201006/10-tips-living-better-life-one-day-time-pope-john-xxiii
[466] http://uacc.arizona.edu/profile/ravitharan-krishnadasan
[467] aplastic anemia and mds foundation
[468] http://makingcancerhistory.com/drdinardo/
[469] http://www.mdanderson.org/about-us/index.html
[470] http://investor.agios.com/phoenix.zhtml?c=251862&p=irol-newsArticle&ID=2120389
[471]

One of the most encouraging aspects of treatment at MD Anderson Cancer Center in Houston is how cancer is viewed in 2016 and how it will be extensively treated in the future. Each cancer is different and a specific medication has to be devised to target the aberrant cells in each. Thus, AG-120 targets the cancerous cells with the IDH-1 [472] mutation in MDS and leukemia, reprogramming them so they become regular white and red blood cells and platelets. It is possible in the next five years, targeted therapies, a genetic approach, will provide solutions to the dreaded "C" word for many types of cancer. Rather than "nuking" cancerous cells, we will change them back into normal cells.

For me, I am still as strong and healthy as a bull moose; Shirley says I am a good caregiver.[473] I lack patience but I still do it. As with many things I've done in life, I muddle through. But one thing all of this has taught me was to think strongly about mortality and how little sand there is left in the upper part of the hourglass.

This writing has been a useful and insightful exercise to think over my life. My memory is very good and I can conjure up minute details about events that happened decades ago. You think back on the things that you did that were downright wrong, sort of wrong, things you said, ways you treated people and say: "But there is no way I can be redeemed." My mouth has always been the cause of most of my trouble. But enumerating these sins and asking forgiveness is a step to redemption, that is, confessing them to God, myself and anyone who reads my story in this book.

I have had strong opinions just about everything, about processes and issues and have been all too willing to publicly announce them, including:

> *Great impatience with the political process in this country, which allows a Presidential campaign to endure almost two years. Why can't we be like the British who accomplish it in about one month with much less money?* [474]
>
> *Cruelty to all animals, whether domestic or wild. Why can't we be kind to all of God's creatures?*
>
> *Rehashing stories ad infinitum. Why can't people tell a story once and remember they told it?*

---

[472] https://en.wikipedia.org/wiki/IDH1
[473] https://en.wikipedia.org/wiki/Caregiver
[474] http://articles.chicagotribune.com/2010-05-14/opinion/ct-oped-0514-british-20100514_1_campaign-spending-candidates-election-day

7-11 music, whether spiritual or popular (7 words and 11 repetitions). Why can't music be more creative?

People who look over your shoulder at a cocktail party to see if they can find someone more interesting with whom to converse. Why is social multi-tasking so prevalent?

Inability of the nation to control gun sales and gun violence because of the Second Amendment. [475] *Why are we so afraid of the NRA?*

Bullying, whether physical, mental, psychological or social. [476] *Why does this happen not only to kids but among adults as well?*

Inability of many to realize there is a difference between private and public behavior? Why can't people keep what they say and do at home at home?

Wine connoisseurs who publicly announce what is acceptable or not to their palate. Why don't they realize the quality of a bottle of wine is mostly provided by what it costs, not how good it is?

Strong opinions like these are indicative of one's pride. I have suffered from having too much most of my life and this is probably my most egregious sin. Of the seven deadly sins, it is the one from which all sins are derived. [477] But PTL. I am working on it. When I hear or sing Joel Hemphill's song, *He's Still Working On Me,* [478] I know redemption is possible:

> *He's still working on me to make me what I ought to be.*
> *It took Him just a week to make the moon and stars,*
> *The sun and the earth, and Jupiter and Mars.*
> *How loving and patient He must be, He's still working on me.* [479].

---

[475] https://en.wikipedia.org/wiki/Second_Amendment_to_the_United_States_Constitution
[476] http://www.apa.org/topics/bullying/
[477] https://en.wikipedia.org/wiki/Seven_deadly_sins
[478] http://www.pine-net.com/~joanbab/hesstill.htm
[479] Hemphill, Joel ©1980

So the train, whether it was car, bus, boat, train or plane does indeed go somewhere. I've experienced many of those places. I've had more experiences and opportunities than I have ever deserved. But I do pray for us, Shirley, Benson and me, there may be many more trains leading to more somewheres. Life goes by so quickly. If you don't grab hold of it each day, it's gone.

You see, it's not really where you go that's important, but that you get up and go. And I have gone. Actually, I have been going all of my life. I have climbed aboard, whether it was train, plane, ship, bus, bike or car and gone. And, without a doubt, every "somewhere" I ended up was well worth it.

Acknowledgements

All successful books require the special eye of someone who did not write it to check grammar, spelling, sentence structure and logical flow. Once again, Shirley, my spouse, was a willing reader and commentator, examining this manuscript several times with an eagle eye to provide a literary flow. I believe I incorporated 99.9% of her corrections and suggestions. The book reads better because of her diligence in forcing me to communicate clearly when I preferred and tended to be pedantic and professorial. Thank you, Shirley, who did this while on our pilgrimage to MD Anderson Cancer Center in Houston, Texas, to enroll and then participate in a clinical trial to mitigate her MDS. The book is a victory for finding the right doctor, the right clinical trial, and the right place to be to conquer this disease as well as the right prayers from an army of global supporters.

I wish to thank all those who offered industrial strength prayers on her behalf, too numerous to list, which provided that spiritual dimension to bring about a 180-degree turn in the treatment of her MDS. Thanks to all the prayer partners.

To this I must add my siblings, Caroline O'Brien Homer, sister, and Thomas M. O'Brien, brother, who not only critiqued this manuscript with diligence and precision, but also corrected my perceptions, facts and narratives, since they were older during all these experiences. Their memories have not failed them. And as I jokingly tell them, they are still older than I. Thanks, Caroline and Tommy. Much like your memories and much like God, you never fail me. And you are very much in this book.

Through all the final writing and editing, while in Houston, Texas, living in our 40-foot motor home, I had a companion animal on my lap or beside me, his head resting on my arm as I tried to key or scroll. Although he is bright enough to run spell check and monitor word usage himself, he mostly provided a warm something beside me to cheer me on when it got tedious, while ever reminding me it was a time to take a break and provide him the mile-walk around the RV resort. Thanks, Benson. You're in the book too.

And I acknowledge God's unfailing support and grace in keeping my memory alive and alert. He wired me with some writing skills so I could convey my narrative to others, whether family, friends or anyone who happens upon this life journey. May the circuitry endure a while longer and may there be something in this book that inspires and encourages whoever reads it.   Carpe diem. [480]

---

[480] https://en.wikipedia.org/wiki/Carpe_diem

Copyright

Cover Photo

Cover photo at Mosier, Oregon ©2006 by Dave Honan, www.davehonan.com.

Let's Get Away From It All

By Matt Dennis and Tom Adair Copyright © 1940 (Renewed) by Onyx Music Corporation All Rights administered by Music Sales Corporation (ASCAP) International Copyright Secured. All rights reserved. Used by permission.

He's Still Working On Me

By Joel Hemphill © 1995 Bridge Building Music (BMI) Family and Friends Music (BMI) (adm. at CapitolCMGPublishing.com) All rights reserved. Used by permission.

About the Author

James P. (Jim) O'Brien spent 42 years as an educator, but retired from the University of Arizona in 2003. He holds the B.S., M.Ed. and Ph.D. in Fine Arts as well as an M.B.A. in marketing and finance. He has also worked as professional tax preparer, real estate agent, land developer, minister of music and professional musician. He completed "Somewhere The Train Goes: A Life Journey" in 2016, based on his life experiences and an incredibly fertile memory. He also completed "Realities of Retirement", based on his beliefs and knowledge about retirement planning in 2015. He has authored 13 books, in total, including two books in music education (Holt, Rinehart and Winston and Prentice-Hall, two in music of global cultures, one in music appreciation with Macmillan (2 editions), as well as instructional manuals.

He lives in a retirement community near Tucson, Arizona, where he and his spouse, Shirley, have written, produced and directed numerous musical shows lampooning senior living in an active, adult retirement community. They spend six months in a 40-foot motor home, primarily on the Oregon coast, as well as six months at their home in Arizona. He is an avid cyclist, walker and pickleball player. The O'Briens continue to perform professionally on digital accordions at festivals and events wherever they are moored, whether in the desert Southwest or the Pacific Northwest.

Made in the USA
San Bernardino, CA
28 July 2016